Introducti

The articles that are stitche... ...g... this book started out as weekly columns for a regional newspaper, The Dundalk Argus. Over a period of almost six years now, they have become a kind of journal of the soul. They reflect my past, my present and my sense of the future. Occasionally they are whimsical or reflective; a wry look at the world from inside the stained glass of the presbytery window. Some readers have persistently encouraged me to put a collection of these columns together. I have tried to arrange those pieces that I have chosen so that they form something of a story, running in chronological order. There are other categories among my collection of columns that I have completely omitted, notably nature or seasonal stories.

Some of the pieces reflect what was going on in my life at a particular time and some contain contemporary references that I have felt should not be edited out. Occasionally they surprise me by the intensity of the feelings that are half-expressed and the topics that were burning issues at the time but that have now passed into the mists of indifference. I am grateful to the former editor of the Dundalk Argus, Kevin Mulligan for trusting me to write on a weekly basis and for giving me that break. Column writing demands intellectual stamina. It can be a demanding art and deadlines help to focus the mind and to sharpen the end-product. I hope that you the reader find something of interest in my story. As my literary poet-hero Patrick Kavanagh once put it, 'The self is interesting only as an illustration'.

Table of Contents

Passport to Heaven

'When did you get the call?' is a question with which most priests will be familiar. Nobody ever asks when you answered the call. At least it's easier to answer than the alternative. 'Why did you become a priest'? 'Have you time to listen'? I generally reply. People generally don't. The question of whether one had a 'call' or not used to be a familiar one in convent and clergy-run secondary schools. This was before the advent of the present bewilderingly wide array of career opportunities. There used to be few options available to those privileged few who made it through to Leaving Certificate or the equivalent. Eldest sons might have been expected to follow in the family tradition or profession. Younger sons might, in distant days, join the armies of their time, become ministers of the church or emigrate. The 'heir and the spare' mentality operated. The options for women were more restricted. A 'call' to religious life often opened up leadership possibilities and responsibilities within society that would otherwise be off limits to women. It was an option taken up by women wholeheartedly during the greater part of the last century. The clerical caste became overwhelmingly dominated by women, at least numerically.

Michael Murtagh

My earliest memory of a serious thought about priesthood was when I attended primary school. We used to deliver the usual missionary magazines to neighbours on our way home through the countryside. At this time, in the early 1960s, the magazines were beginning to show pictures of newly professed black nuns and priests. At school we had listened to heroic stories and adventures of missionaries in Africa. The idea of vocation was held in high honour generally. Myself and my female companion, while meandering along the way home from school, decided we would be a priest and a nun respectively. There was a slight problem though. We decided to be a black priest and a black nun! It was harvest time of the year and being resourceful we found a solution, a temporary one at least. We gathered some blackberries, squashed them between our fingers and stained our faces, only our faces, black. There was a long lane up to our house and a mother who hadn't seen anyone for the greater part of the day at the end of it. Imagine her surprise when she saw a black-faced child at the door. 'Surely', she must have thought, 'he was white when I sent him out this morning'. There was little in the way of facilities at the time. I was taken to the water tub and the idea of vocation was scrubbed out of me for a long time, along with the stubborn blackberry stains.

I later attended a 'junior seminary' as our secondary school was officially designated. We were taught by priests and these undoubtedly influenced some of us. Having resurrected my dormant 'call' I wrote to a vocations director who replied to me that the best thing to do at my premature age was to attend a junior seminary. I wrote back asking where the nearest one to me was and he replied that, being a boarder, I was already living in it! I later chose a different future for myself, left school and entered the world of work and commerce. Five years later, a sequence of events led me to reconsider my dormant sense of vocation. Lazarus was called forth again. Living had matured me a little. It had changed and re-directed me and events had made me more thoughtful and reflective about how I might spend my life. I had finally 'got the call.' I became a 'late vocation' at the age of twenty-two. This is a term I find ironic for one like myself who is obsessively early.

In later years I found myself studying with priests from Africa. I now find myself sharing my home and my work with a black African priest. I have long held the belief that God has an ironic, even a perverse sense of humour. It has been said that there are moments in childhood that open a window on to the future of that person. The day that I covered my freckles with blackberry stain was surely my epiphany. There are few periods of twenty years, such as the intervening two decades, in which so much has changed. The days of over-supply of clergy with the consequent over-mannning of parishes and the phenomenon of family dynasties of clerics has gone. The very notion of voluntary service to any ideal, never mind lifetime vocation to church ministry, has all but collapsed. The evidence is in the decline of interest in the twin 'secular' vocations of nursing and teaching and in the decline of interest in political and voluntary societies. Prosperity appears to exact a social price.

The pedestal of priestly life has been turned into an occasional pillory. Instant, mostly unrealistic and unhelpful solutions are suggested from the liberal left and much proposed reform, is of the 'back to the future' variety and is coming mostly from the rigid right. The profile of the student priest has changed beyond recognition. The fault lines and fragilities of society are now reflected in the few candidates that come forward. The academic excellence that used to be necessary for entry to seminary has been all but abandoned. 'Late' vocations, often touted as the answer to human development deficiencies or immaturity among clergy, are no guarantee of maturity or of perseverance. Age or experience is no guarantee that the individual has learned or can benefit from having lived.

The only thing certain in the future is that change, chosen or otherwise, will continue and will continue to accelerate. As the present decline had taken place over a generation now, the process of regeneration, when it begins, will also take several decades. The 'call' is always mediated through the prevailing culture and changing that culture, altering the values of a generation, reclaiming the radical response for religious vocation, is always difficult. After all a 'call' will remain just that, an unanswered 'call' without the marriage of a response.

In the beginning...

Around 1960 when I was two years old, my family moved from a two-up, two-down, Coronation Street type terrace of houses in Banbridge to a small farm on the Armagh-Monaghan border. My father gave up his manager's job in the licensed trade in favour of the, 'good life' of farming sixteen acres on the Western side of a South Armagh drumlin. The farm had been recently inherited from my mother's bachelor uncle, a blacksmith-farmer straight out of the pages of Kavanagh's Tarry Flynn. The farm was burdened by debt and legacies but the lately deceased, in a fit of masculine thoughtfulness, had left one kicking cow, 'to feed the childer'. The bovine herd eventually grew to six milking cows. Six breeding sows, a farm horse, a few dozen chickens and sundry farm pets constituted the whole live population of the holding at its height.

The animals were treated with an intimacy of sorts. The farm horse was regarded as an auxiliary family member. The cows and sows had their pet names. Only the chickens on their perch remained aloof and anonymous. Great interest was taken in the breeding cycles of the stock and great sorrow was expressed in their tragedies. The methods of animal husbandry and the general standard of farming were primitive. It had probably changed little since medieval times, like the wheel-less slipe drawn by the horse over the sodden, heavy 'wet bottoms' of the meadows; what Kavanagh called the 'rushy beards' that took the run-off from the steep small hills.

In time the Ferguson T20 tractor replaced the farm horse. Piped water made the well redundant. A flush toilet and bathroom was installed and push-button technology arrived in the form of a cumbersome wireless. The threshing mill continued to provide harvest-time theatre and a sense of mutual dependence among the neighbours. The diet was adequate if deficient in variety. Electricity remained an aspiration.

A decade later the whole fabric of the smallholding culture was unravelling. By that time my father had drifted back into paid employment in the licensed trade and our family of five plus two had migrated to the village. My mother had taken a job as a carer to elderly residents in a housing scheme. The later acquisition of ten more acres proved to be no incentive to return to the land. The future lay in regular and well-paid employment. Farming was becoming a sideline occupation. The apparently timeless, seasonal rhythm of the countryside was giving way to the more regulated, energy-efficient, maximum-producing cycles of industry and commerce. The leisure culture of countryside ceilidhing was giving way to the culture of the Lounge Bar. The industrialisation of farming life had begun. A flight from the land had set in. Valleys that had previously been, in the words of one farmer, 'shaking with work' fell silent but for the lazy lowing of low-maintenance suckler herds, subsidised by the European Union. Townlands emptied. Homesteads crumbled into damp, desolate dumping places.

Some of these former full-time farmers moved no further than the nearest village, keeping the smallholding as an annual bonus to their welfare payments or to an industrial wage. Some took the boat, or increasingly, the aeroplane. The young, intoxicated by new educational opportunities, dreamt dreams and sprouted wings that took them to high places and far shores to heights never aspired to by previous generations. Farmland stagnated without the regular sharp surgery of the plough. Some farms were amalgamated and had their hedgerows ripped. Seamless fields were turned into large, efficient (though subsidised) industrial units, producing the cheapest possible food for the supermarket and capable of handling huge farm machinery driven by solitary operators.

The old ways of farming and the culture of the countryside so realistically portrayed in the writings of Patrick Kavanagh have all but vanished. The dynamic of how people relate to each other has been utterly changed in the whole process of greater urbanisation. We have become not interdependent but increasingly independent and isolated. The old dispensation was far from romantic but it had its compensations. Equally shattered is the dream of the industrialist model of farming and the rules of the free marketeers. Food and beverages are undoubtedly more varied, more available and more consumed but the inevitable kickback is the advent of the modern plague, viruses that slip through the scientific net because of cost cutting. These include salmonella, mad-cow, and now foot and mouth. These viruses or diseases defy modern scientific technology. They can poison the food chain and ruin the fragile tourist industry. Nature has its own integrity and we ignore it at our peril. We remain vulnerable. As the Guard said to me at the 'foot and mouth' checkpoint on the border yesterday, 'Only God and his Blessed Mother can keep it out now'.

Michael Murtagh

Commodity Relocation

One of my earliest memories is of waking in what seemed to me to be the dead of night to the sound of squealing pigs. Having been reared on a farm it was a sound I was accustomed to. These nocturnal noises came not from our own herd housed out in the 'street', but from the slippery backs of the Morris Minor vans which regularly travelled the border road that ran past the perimeter of our holding. We bordered on county Monaghan. The road ran or rather lurched at a right angle to our laneway and then swung left into a valley. In the valley, between two of the many lakes which dotted the drumlinned landscape, ran a drain which marked the border. The road swung right up the steep incline of the neighbouring drumlin and into county Monaghan. It is a remote stretch of road and was used frequently by smugglers of livestock, of dry goods or of whatever was being moved from one jurisdiction to another at any given time. This was commodity relocation as it later became euphemistically labelled, or cross-border co-operation, South Armagh style.

The economy of the whole area was often subsidised by this exchange of goods one way or another back and forward across the border.

The area had been ripe for the development of this black economy. It had what would now be described as an educated workforce in the dealers and jobbers who had long worked their trade buying and selling hens, calves, cattle and pigs. The associations of the area with dealing had been documented in poem and song long before the border provided the opportunity for business expansion. A culture of song and storytelling built around the evasion of customs and excise and of officialdom had taken root. The dealing men from Crossmaglen had been putting whiskey in the tea of innocents long before a stream became the border not between two counties but between two parts of the same country. The road from Crossmaglen into Carrickmacross had become known, affectionately of course, as the abode of rogues and it was said to be scarce of honest men. 'Paveying' or casual dealing in all and any kind of goods had been common in the area long before cross-border smuggling or the drawing of the border which made it possible.

The professional jobbers, guinea hunters and dealers were a class apart. These were not the paveys or hucksters whose job was once described as, 'selling small goods to the rubbish of the country'. The professionals, the 'fair green gods' as Kavanagh called them had an air of authority and an arcane code worthy of any professional. The outward signs of their office were their neck-tie or cravat, worn inside the open shirt neck and usually brightly coloured. They wore the standard yellow leather boots that became fashionable in later years and they carried a carefully prepared and well seasoned wooden warrior-type walking stick topped off with a copper ferrule. They spoke in their own verbal code of things like bainíns (white, almost worthless calves), of scroofies, (maimed or damaged cattle), of poleing, (artificially inflating the cost of cattle at auction by bidding on your own stock), and of having stripes, (commissions to buy stock for another). They spoke of travelling to fairs and marts well beyond their native locality and they exchanged information about trade and opportunities. They had their trade specialities, one trading in dairy stock, another in calves, another in butchers' heifers and so on. Though most of them were men it was not exclusively a men's club.

There was also the more local opportunistic smuggler using the occasion of wartime scarcity or the periodic inequality of prices North and South to save some money rather than to make a living or to amass a fortune. Women tailored their dresses to conceal small amounts of butter, eggs or whatever was in demand. Some enterprising smugglers did make fortunes. Many lost their hard won fortunes through mismanagement or alcohol. An older, World War Two generation remembers the smuggling opportunities which rationing and wartime scarcities brought about. Cigarettes and alcohol became smuggling staples and in later years, heating oil and fossil fuels. Citizen Band radios and mechanised bulk transport transformed smuggling from the woman smuggling a few pounds of butter to the entrepreneur with modern communications equipment and transport moving bulk quantities of goods across the border according to the direction of the economic tide.

The culture which made smuggling possible had been created by the economic and social conditions of the area. South of the Mournes was not a good place to be within Northern Ireland. Industry and Tourism were virtually non-existent and the income from farms often had to be supplemented by part-time activities and jobs, or local crafts like Carrickmacross lace making. The border created new opportunities in the two different economies and currencies which came to exist, in the differing laws operating in each jurisdiction and later still, in the European Union subsidies for farming. Politicians drawing lines through communities, through farms, through lakes and eventually through the hearts of people found that they had created an economic backwater, a people who felt betrayed and politically abandoned by their southern counterparts. They had created an economic underclass, a crushed community who fought back economically by 'jumping' the border which sought to fence them in. The Irish attitude to law that had developed over centuries of colonial rule was one of seeing law as a challenge, the challenge being to circumvent it.

Soap gets in your eyes

'Saturday night and not a child in the house washed'! This used to be a common saying in Irish households when Saturday evening rituals included the weekly bath for the children of the house, if not for the adults. This was in the days when showers all happened outside, when you didn't have control of the on/off taps and when the weather dictated the temperature of the water. Indoor, improvised baths were the only alternative to a summer dip in the nearest lake or stream. The water for the bath had to be heated, usually on an open fire or on a 'range.' Kettles full of steaming water were needed to half-fill the tin bath on the kitchen floor. The bath was generally placed strategically near the fire that had heated the water. There was little sense of privacy. All of this heating of water, testing the temperature and cooling it with cold water took time and effort. Most of Saturday evening was taken up with these preparations and with the subsequent washing of the 'childer'.

It was occasionally interrupted by the arrival of the bread-man on his twice-weekly visit. This meant the pleasing possibility of getting first read at the 'Dandy' and the adventures of Desperate Dan. The adults got the weekly newspaper. It might also mean the treat of a cube-like, Madeira sticky-bun with coconut shavings on top or one dusted with small, multicoloured 'hundreds and thousands'. It also gave us the sights and scents of freshly-baked batch-loaves. These were drawn forward with a long, wooden implement by the friendly bread-man from deep down the shelf of the van.

The bath was generally a long, shallow tin container with two grips, one at either end. When the mix of water was thought to be at the right temperature, the ritual bathing began. If you were lucky, you were given a bar of what my grandmother used to call 'scinty' soap with which to prise off the grime. This perfumed or scented soap was so called to distinguish it from the less sudsy block of red or green carbolic soap that was used for washing clothes. It had a distinctly disinfectant-type smell.

The row then began as to who would be 'first in'. This was a delicate decision. You had to balance the benefits of the first dip in the clean, hot water with the probability that your stay in the tub would be shorter than that of those who followed you. The decision might be made for you if you happened to suffer from any wound or sore that might infect the others so you were relegated to 'last in'. Being last into the bath was a mixed blessing. The water was generally softer and soapier and you might get a longer stay as mother dried and buffed the earlier bathers. The temperature was generally lukewarm by then and the floor of the tin tub was gravelled by discarded dust and obscured by the shedding of a week's accumulated debris from several siblings. On giving up occupancy of the tub mother checked that each child was properly washed by examining and scrubbing behind the ears and on the back of the hard-neck and occasionally a bather was forced back into the tub - for real washing this time rather than for splashing and fun.

Our parents, having filled topped-up and emptied the bath tub, the battle then began among the 'childer' for places around the fire or the stove. Towels were useful not only for drying and for keeping the shivers at bay. They could also be used as whips. A 'rat's tail' could be formed by folding the towel diagonally so that a narrow strip of the towel formed a long thin, tail-like weapon. This could be used to stinging effect on the bare skin of those who invaded your space. When pecking order had been established, parental instructions then went out for night-wear and for bed-time. Bathing was a refreshing experience and the hot water inevitably left us thirsty and hungry so supper had to be negotiated first.

This ritual of Saturday-night preparation was repeated all across the country in the days before widespread electrification or Saturday evening Mass. It was part of a more detailed set of tasks that were particular to Saturday night. The scuffed shoes of the family members, or more likely, their boots, had to be cleaned of their accumulated mud before they were polished and lined up neatly like a row of soldiers, ready for inspection and for morning duty. The job of polishing the footwear generally fell to the father of the household, especially when the family were younger. Mother polished the children to a squeaky, shiny finish, having earlier starched their Sunday shirts and smooth-ironed their pants with razor-sharp creases. Meanwhile father buffed their footwear and kept the fire fuelled.

Next morning we lined up in front of the small, swivel-mirror that creaked with age as it was adjusted in its wooden frame. It was almost the full of the old sash-window in the kitchen. Father opened the Brylcreem, set aside the lid and inserted his index finger in the greasy jar. He then plopped a dollop of the contents on to the tousle of hair on each of our boyish heads. He followed up by running all of his ten, big, work-hardened fingers through our hair, massaging our scalps and distributing the scented grease. A quick run of a communal, hairy brush was enough to whip our shiny fringes stickily into place and we were ready for Mass. After Mass came the visit to grandmother's well-kept house for dinner and for the weekly delight of custard and jelly.

As a family we improved our lot as time went on and we graduated to piped, running water and then to hot water generated by a solid-fuel range or cooker. A bathroom was built and the enamelled bath arrived. Later still came the indoor electric shower and more frequent bathing habits. In the local leisure centre I now enjoy the warm bubbly jacuzzi, the moist heat of the steam room and the sweaty challenge of the high-temperature sauna followed by a cold, (indoor!) shower. The rituals of contemporary Saturday nights have changed as has the conformity and the communal nature of life in the countryside and towns of those times. Saturday night now has me wondering what I'm going to say to the tired benches of faithful worshippers who turn up at Sunday Mass or what I'm going to inflict on readers of the Argus next Wednesday morning. I wonder what Saturday night family rituals future generations will remember from the early years of the Millennium

Michael Murtagh

Escape into freedom

I recently attended the funeral of a former primary teacher who taught me for four years, 1965-1969. She was an awesome character. We pupils had been told of her, even warned about her in those less politically correct times as we made our way through the first half of a two teacher school deep in the country at Anamar, half way between Crossmaglen and Cullyhanna. I'm not sure if she ever knew her power over us and her ability to form minds and to influence behaviour. She was a strong person. She was confident, assertive and capable, like the best of her liberated successors. She was deeply traditional too, steeped in the spirituality of the time. She was also revolutionary in the way she utilised the educational system to work out her vision of how the sectarian society we lived in could be changed.

The 11plus exam was the bane of our young lives but ultimately it was to become our escape into freedom. We began studying for it several years before our eleventh birthday and we worked the test sheets until we were achieving an average of 85% correct. Passing it meant access to government grants which would enable us to go boarding or to grammar schools. Nobody in our immediate families, in our locality, or in our smallholding society had dreamed of such things before. Few, or none of our parents had even second level education. Because of a British Education Act, a talented and visionary teacher and a bit of hard work, all this was to change.

There is a theory that the access to good second level education which was promised by the education act, ultimately led to the crisis in Northern Ireland in the late 1960s. Because of the introduction of the act in the 1940s, the theory goes, and allowing for the time it took the first graduates of the 11plus to make their way through college and university, the graduates who emerged constituted a new kind of grouping. Catholics from backgrounds which were not professional or business class suddenly began to make their way through these colleges and universities and onto the political stage and to articulate the grievances of their people, especially from the early 1960s. Education had set them free or was promising to. 'We shall overcome' was their catch-cry.

There was a new class of student emerging in the boarding school I later attended. A group of about thirty five boarders from Crossmaglen area all stood out and spoke out like gatecrashers. There was also an influx from Belfast and from other troubled Northern areas that had been sent by their parents to the safety and seclusion of boarding school. There was the majority whose parents and grandparents had attended the school and who still had access to a tradition of study, education and excellence and there were we, 'johnny come latelies' with none of the usual middle-class baggage. This told against us. Most failed to take full advantage of the opportunities and only a tiny percentage completed the course and went on to university. There was a culture among us which said that work was more important than education and which could not imagine or sustain the long years of study among strangers which was needed to graduate. We simply lacked social confidence.

What happened subsequently is well documented. Access to education is now not only available more freely but taken up more freely too. I think that my former teacher would be glad to think that she was at the cutting edge of a new dispensation. Her sense of justice would be satisfied and her distaste for injustice vindicated. Teachers face new pressures and new conditions and injustices. They still have profound opportunities for influencing their charges and helping to change society. I believe that despite the utter change in social conditions, a good teacher with a vision which can be worked can still change the course of events within and among persons. Come the revolution!

Michael Murtagh

Up the 'house'

He's gone to school, wee Hughie, and he just four.... The sentimental old poem summed up the feelings of parents and pupils as school began for the first time or resumed after the summer break. Over forty years ago I made that first journey to school on my fourth birthday. Primary school was a small two-teacher school in the heart of the countryside, in a place called Anamar, now famous as the birth place of the late Cardinal Ó Fiaich. There were only thirty something of us at any given time during those early years. The youngest of us were driven there in the morning. All of us walked home in the evening. The journey home could be just as instructive as the school lessons. We learned a lot about nature as we explored the hedgerows and streams and we learned something of human nature too as we interacted on the homeward journey. Life got progressively more serious as we moved up the ranks from P1 to P7. The last few years were spent cramming for the 11plus exam.

Having passed the 11plus some of us arrived at boarding school in Saint Colman's, Newry: otherwise known as Violet Hill, armed with a sheaf of government grants, our passport to 'grammar' school'. I got off to a bad start by taking a detour to Daisy Hill Hospital on the night of my first full day, suffering from appendicitis. I owe my life to a priest who had been expelled from Nigeria where the Biafran war was then raging, and who was now teaching in a temporary capacity in the college. He was the only one who believed that my pain was anything more than travel sickness or homesickness. It was 1969 and the North was in turmoil. I arrived in hospital having made my way through Bessbrook to avoid the burning in Newry town centre that night. I resumed school a few weeks later as a boarder.

I boarded there from 1969 to 1975, with the exception of one year as a day-boy. We used to write our address as Violent Hill when we were writing letters. The president, as the priest-principal was called, was not impressed by our verbal juggling. In truth, it was not especially violent, but there were rules of survival and it may have been more violent for some than for others. The only reason my older brother and I attended there was because we had passed the 11 plus exam and were given grants to attend 'grammar' school. A group from South Armagh began to attend, to the annoyance of many better bred and highly polished sons of college old boys, mostly middle class professionals. Our parents visited us occasionally in big Austin Cambridge workhorse cars or, in Morris Minor vans with straw still dangling from the back doors, while their parents swept or cruised up the long avenue in Saabs, Volvos and B.M.W's. We spoke with a different accent, our hobbies were different, and even our footballing interest differed, we not being much into English League.

The regime was strict. The daily horarium had probably not changed since the college was founded by Rev John Sproule Keenan who had left his classical academy in Dundalk to found it in the 1820s. We rose at seven, washed (in cold water), cleaned, prayed, breakfasted, went to school from 9.00-3.30, recreation until 5pm, then first study period in two large assembly rooms, followed by tea at 6.30, rosary at 7.30, followed by second study, night prayer at 9.30, followed by bedtime, lights out and solemn silence. Recreation meant football or handball. We were allowed to see a film twice a month from which we returned, ducking and driving and shooting at each other up and down banisters and along corridors.

Discipline was strict but seldom overdone in my experience. Leather straps were the official weapons. Priest teachers kept these in a mysterious inner pocket on their winged soutanes. They would throw the wings back and hold their soutane cuffs in one hand to brush chalk off somewhere else with it. Most of them were benign though there was one or two we avoided because of their temper or for some other unspoken and mysterious reason that we did not quite understand. In the 1970s following the second Vatican council and the social upheaval of the 1960s, many of the priest teachers disappeared. We didn't ask questions and it was years later I realised that many of them had left the priesthood during the exodus of that time.

I still remember my feelings of despondency as I made my way back to school over the next five or six years. Being a boarder, I travelled home every six weeks so going back to school after a weekend break at home could be traumatic. I can still visualise the lights of Newry in the hollow as we arrived from the Camlough road on a Sunday night. I can still smell the interior of the lockers that we used to hoard our apples and cheese and 'Marvel' dried milk for our cereals. We also brought eggs, jam, and sugar to sweeten our daily diet. Soon we settled back into routine and began counting down the days of another term. People ask me sometimes whether I think it was a good or a bad experience for a young student. We entered at eleven years of age. It was certainly deficient in terms of what might now be termed the inner life of a child. Little emotional or pastoral care was evident. What was available was well disguised. The emotional landscape was more desert than oasis. The benefits it did offer were discipline in life and in study and an ability to care for and organise yourself. It was a television-free routine, with none of the distractions of home or of the outside world. We spoke of the college as the 'house' but there were few of the comforts of home. I left the 'house' during the first term of my 'A' Levels, abandoning my studies of English, Irish and Spanish. I believed that I had left school for the final time.

Six years later I went back to school. I entered Maynooth only to discover that 'Colmans' had been merely a pale imitation of the master pattern in Kildare. I was twenty two years of age and I was going back to school. The language of the 'house' remained but the terms of our course of education had changed. We 'read' rather than studied philosophy. Instead of compositions we submitted assignments. We had professors instead of teachers. We prepared theses instead of essays and we had seminars in place of study groups. There was still solemn silence at night time, in theory at least but study was no longer communal. In secondary school we had two study periods each evening, 'first steed' and 'second steed'. These lasted for over three hours. Now we were expected to study alone. At first I thought this university business might be beyond me but I soon realised that like most 'mature students' I was highly motivated and I soon fell into the routine of 'Third Level'. I left six years later thinking that this was definitely the end of going back to school. Six years later I went back to school. This time I studied full time during the Summer months and part time during the rest of the year for a period of three years. I experienced the trauma of unfinished assignments and 'comprehensive' exams all over again. I also knew the joy of learning as an adult.

I have long wondered what the advantages and disadvantages of boarding school were for me. We always spoke of the college as 'the house' yet it was far from the comforts and intimacy of a house. We refer to our old college as our 'alma mater', our other mother, yet there was little motherly care. The only female directly looking after us was an elderly nun who took charge of the infirmary. Though she had one of those strange Greek-sounding religious names, she was known among us as 'bulldog'. Enough said.

Back to school is no longer the prerogative of the young and staying at school for much longer than in the past has become the norm.

Education, teaching and schools may have their problems yet education is still highly prized. Primary school children generally love their schools and teachers. The fear and distance of the old ways is largely gone, unmissed and unmourned. There is a spring in Wee Hughie's step nowadays as he sets out to school.

Gone fishing

Every time I turn over a sod or upturn a stone from its damp-underneath and uncover a large earthworm of the kind called a 'blackhead' my inclination is to imprison it immediately in a jam-jar or in a tin can. This spontaneous reaction arises from my childhood pastime of fishing in the lakes that gathered around the base of the drumlins where I was brought up. There was little by way of in-house entertainment on summer evenings then so we took to the great outdoors and went fishing. The lakes were generally considered dangerous so we went under supervision until we had earned the trust of our parents. In mid-summer it was possible to fish into the late evening. We often ended an evening's fishing because we could no longer see the floats on the surface of the lake. By then it was usually rippling a little more than earlier as the night breeze rose.

Our earliest equipment consisted of a simple bamboo pole about six feet long and some strong fishing line attached securely to the top of it. This was then equipped with a float that was placed about three or four feet above the end of the line. The float might be an egg-shaped plastic one with a brightly coloured top and a white base. This was pierced through by a tapered plastic wedge that looked like a lollipop-stick with a loop at the top or an elongated, more sophisticated version of the same with wire loops at top and bottom. At its most basic we used a cork that had been bored lengthways through the centre and we plugged it with a stick that had been chosen carefully from the blossoming hedges. I had an elderly cousin who owned a pub and who was an avid fisherman. He stored corks from the pub in white stone-bags during the winter time and gave them out liberally to us during the fishing season. Once the float was attached the hook was withdrawn carefully from its mooring on yet another cork. With eyes carefully focused, the fishing line was threaded through the eye of the hook and tied. This is where the worm suffered.

The task of gathering bait for the fishing expedition used to take place during the day until we got more skilled and learned that night-time was worm-time. Blackheads were highly prized for the kind of coarse fishing we indulged in. We dug a patch in the garden until we had filled an improvised bait-box or jar with many more worms than we ever expected to catch fish. If the supply of worms was measly we opted for the second-best source which was the dung-hill. There was always a ready supply of thinner, redder worms in the rotting compost but they were not easy to put on a hook or to keep securely there. They were apparently not as attractive to the fish as their clay-bound, larger cousins with their pink flesh and trademark saddle. I understood why. As our knowledge increased we learned to leave out wet sacks overnight to attract the worms or to use detergent to annoy them to the surface or simply to go out at night with a flash-lamp.

When we had an adequate or generous supply of worms squirming frothily in the bottom of the jar we added a little fine clay to keep them in good shape for the hunt. It was important not to add too much lest the worms reach the top of the jar and slide their way out again. No fisherman liked to discover escaped worms in the bottom of his canvas bag. The trick was to use a screw-top jam-jar with a crudely perforated ceiling. Having reached the intended location, we secured a good place on the bank and tackled up. The finest specimen of worm was extracted following a selection process of rolling and shaking the jar and then using two fingers in a pincer movement. This could take several attempts as the jar was narrow and the worms were reluctant. If all else failed, the jar was gently emptied into the left palm and with fingers held tightly closed the unselected were returned to their glass prison to hope for a poor catch that night. At night's end these unused bait were often tossed into the water, followed perhaps by the empty jar.

The selected worm was carefully threaded on to the vicious hook until it was secured. If it was a blackhead, the thick saddle of flesh was often used as an anchor for the hook as it tore less easily. The portion of the line between the hook and the float was sometimes weighted with a lead-shot. These were small, graded pellets of lead that had been cut half-open. They were pressed onto the line with pliers or, less healthily or hygienically, with one's strong front teeth, leaving a dentist's impression on them in the process. The lead helped the fisherman to cast out and to keep the float anchored, with the bait at the correct depth. The amount of lead used was carefully computed, as too much could sink the float or make it less sensitive to a 'bite'. The cast-out was not always completed on first attempt. If the worm had been badly attached, or the cast-out was unduly awkward, the worm might be lost and the process of attaching another worm-bait had to start all over again. The worst result was not to notice the worm escaping from the flying hook and to sit patiently and fruitlessly, becoming dizzy watching a bait-less hook and an ever-bobbing float. After some time the float usually drifted to one side or another, nearer to the shore-line or to some obstacle and the process of drawing in, checking and then casting out began all over again.

As time and technology progressed we graduated to fibreglass fishing rods and to fishing reels. These were capable of carrying metal or plastic fishing lures or the traditional hook and worm further out into the lake. They also enabled greater accuracy in casting and targeting. It also meant that the mighty pike could be tackled. The usual take was a few small perch, an occasional eel, especially if we were trawling the floor of the lake and sometimes an elusive roach. These skitted tantalizingly on the lake surface on warm evenings tempting one to forsake rod and reel and dive in among them. They were bony creatures but they put up a good fight – a little like ourselves.

Eels could be similarly troublesome if they had time to wind themselves around the base of the reeds and bullrushes that grew along the shoreline. They were elusive even when landed as they did not die quickly or easily. They could slip out of a fishing bag, escape through the grass like a snake, leaving only their dried slime-track on the palms. The trick apparently was to have some sand or salt to affect a firm grip, to kill the fish by almost beheading it, to skin it by holding the barely-attached head, then rolling off the skin as if removing a sock. The discarded skin was said to be a cure for sprained wrists or, in bygone days, for tying the two sticks together that went to make up a flail. Fishermen came from Ardboe in County Tyrone to fish the lakes commercially for these eels - but that's another story. It's a long time now since I fished regularly but my childhood conditioning means that I can never see a worm simply as a worm.

Hairy Apples

It only happens occasionally but the residents of Crossmaglen have gone orange and its not orange lilies they are sporting. It has nothing to do with the marching season either. There is orange bunting, orange flags and orange paraphernalia all over the place. There are orange jerseys, orange baseball caps and orange kit bags. Anything that can be coloured orange is available except collarettes.

It is not often that 'Cross' gets a chance to show its true colours. Of course the amber and black of the local Rangers G.F.C. is a much better seller and a more dependable bet in recent years. 'Cross' reveals its wider identity only when the team, now under a native manager, Joe Kernan, manages to get to the Ulster final or beyond. Of course we all know that Cross is part of South Armagh. Anywhere in Armagh is part of South Armagh when there is trouble to report. The parish is a bit more inclusive. It takes in a bit of Louth; Shelagh, the bit that used to be termed the 'ten towns of the Fews'. The Fews is an ancient territorial name that covered a lot of South Armagh and a bit of what is now Louth. The parish properly known as Upper Creggan consists of two different counties, two different provinces and two different international jurisdictions, now with different currencies.

'From time to time, something like madness takes possession of a district... until they become a byeword. Among the districts having attained this unenviable fame was the district of Crossmaglen in County Armagh.' The Attorney General, Abraham Brewster delivered himself of the above quote at Monaghan assizes in 1853. He was not the only one to cast aspersions on the reputation of 'Cross'. The deputy Inspector General of the police had said something similar the year before. He took care to say it in London during a government enquiry. There had been talk then of 'Cross' as a stain on the fair empire and in recent years the epithet 'Bandit Country' took hold. The locals wisely pointed out that the real bandits were the name callers.

Armagh is widely known by the title of the Orchard County. This used to puzzle me greatly. I was reared, though not born, in South Armagh and the only apple trees I knew of were two ancient crab-apple trees at the bottom of our lane. The apple orchards from which the county takes its nickname are a feature of North Armagh and are all but missing from the southernmost parts of the county. It was only as I grew older and moved around the county that I discovered evidence of the, 'orchard of Erin's green land' as the county anthem puts it.

As a youngster I remember accompanying my late father to football matches, especially Ulster finals in Clones. Cavan and Down, the latter being my county of birth, were in the ascendancy then. I remember little of the football but I remember the strange new experiences that came with a visit to Clones, the football Mecca of Monaghan. A particular, personal disappointment stands out in my memory. There always seemed to be large itinerant women at the matches heaving huge straw baskets of fruit and chocolate, selling them among the crowd. My eyes were feasting on the peaches that were piled at the side of one lady's basket. I didn't know the proper name for them. I thought they were some special variety of apples. When I asked for one of those apples, (I meant the hairy ones) and pointed to the side of the basket, the lady looked puzzled and handed me a big smooth red apple from the centre. I admitted defeat and enjoyed the fruit of the orchard anyway.

It was easier to support Down in the 1960s. They won the national title in 1960, 1961 and in 1968. When I entered Saint Colman's College in Newry, (the football factory of County Down) in September 1969 the Sam Maguire was still in Down's possession. I remember one small first year student being placed inside the cup for a photograph. Armagh came good in 1977 after a semi-final replay with Roscommon but they fell to Dublin in a forgettable, (for Armagh) final. I attended these games. My kinsman, Tom Mc Creesh was nearing the end of an honourable football career then and Joe Kernan was young, slim and in full flight.

I recall bringing a sealed saucepan of Irish stew and a camper stove with me in the car boot. I heated the stew and entered Croke Park with my hunger satisfied. It was easier to take defeat on a full stomach. What was not easy to take was the message that awaited me. I had parked carefully but I was too near one local resident's driveway for her comfort. When I arrived back at the car there was a message written in red lipstick on my car windscreen telling me in terms that were not uncertain, never to park near to her driveway again. I didn't get the chance in recent years but maybe the day is coming when I can return and undo my indiscretion, and celebrate by eating some 'hairy apples'.

The generous impulse

'Throw an extra bale to the cattle', my father used to tell us in later life as we set out to fodder the family stock. We remembered the tradition from childhood. I used to wonder what the cattle made of this sudden impulse of generosity. Did they think it was going to last? Were they disappointed when rations went back to normal next day? What sort of feast was this, I wondered to myself, where even the animals shared in the general and generous good will?

Christmas then, or now, wasn't as kind to the poultry of course. The roosters that had eaten Christmas rations for several months and who had reached ten or twelve pounds weight were about to eat the last meal of the condemned. Their rations were then cut off abruptly for a day or so before their death, 'to empty their craw' before killing, plucking, cleaning-out, stuffing and roasting in someone else's oven. Some Christmas they had!

Country people used to say that the animals knelt down in the byre on Christmas Eve. This was on account of the animals' privilege of being represented in the stable as the divine child was born in the manger. This gesture of bowing or kneeling didn't apply to the out-wintered cattle. It was simply too cold or too wet for cattle out in the fields to be pious. The stall-fed cows nosed around in their evening-filled mangers, blowing misty breaths, radiating body warmth, and slowly filling up their slackened udders with morning milk. What they got up to or down to at midnight, no one checked. Faith provides. Anyway, we were all at Mass by then.

We knew Christmas was near when the aptly named Fr Halpenny had opened the parish bazaar. Three discs like dartboards were set up high on the parish hall stage and the raffles were decided on their spin. The spinning discs clicked their suspense-filled way to a halt. Ticket numbers were called, checked and confirmed. A half-tin of biscuits or a bottle of port? Decisions, decisions. The glinting prizes piled up on the glitter-scattered stage provided a foretaste of the season's promise and generosity. They slowly made their way into the hands of the lucky winners who were congratulated at the end of the evening on their good fortune and their willingness to part with their money, gambling for the good of the parish.

Alcohol made a rare and seasonal visit to many homes. Half-dozens of frothy black stout and naggins of golden 'Powers' packaged in stout stone-bags were half hidden between the dresser and the corner of the room. One bottle of stout was sacrificed for the pudding, and maybe a trickle of whiskey for the cake. It was a poor and ungenerous house or host that didn't have a 'trate' to offer (along with a bit of silver) to wet the tongue of the very-much-expected postman. As we approached the final days, the 'jaws of Christmas' we children were taken on a visit to the maiden aunt who kept house for the priest on the northern side of the parish. For some unexplained reason, Santa always previewed at her house. She must have been 'well-in' with him. She showed us the dent he made in the bucket that he had stood on to allow himself reach and enter the open window. Hers was a practical Santa. He left toys certainly but there was always a supply of freshly knitted warm woollen jumpers as well. They do things strangely in the farther end of the parish.

Midnight Mass was the final hurdle before the night of suspense and surprises. We children knelt, like the animals, our eyes heavy with sleep, full of wonder, mostly as to when Mass would be over. The ritual ended, we visited the crib under the gallery stairs. Grandmother took a piece of straw from the bedding of the sacred scene, cut it with her nail and forefinger and faith-fully folded it into her purse, 'for good luck'.

We returned home, drove into the 'street' and waited in the car for my father to light the gas lamp in the kitchen. He struck a match to see his way, found and pulled the shorter chain marked 'on', listened for the hiss of the gas and deftly held the flame of a lit match below the delicate mantle. It glowed a warm custard colour, brightened to primrose yellow and lit our way in from the car, straight to our respective sides of our beds. No arguing tonight. We processed obediently like cows to their stalls.

Our drowsy, sand-filled eyes soon closed in sleep and opened a little stickily and much later in the morning than planned. Soon the Christmas morning air was sulphurous with smoke from cowboy rifles and cap-guns. 'You can't shoot a running tiger' I protested as I ran from the cover of the wardrobe, dived and took up position just around the door-jamb. We were an all boys herd. It made for a boisterous Christmas morning, dodging the shots of waist-coated, western, rival siblings, cowboys all. The morning battles over, we older ones helped my father as he did the 'turns' and fed the cattle their extra lot. I imagined their pious bowing and kneeling of the previous night. Extra rations were their reward for the homage paid and duty done to the Christ child. Long after all else has changed, this God-led generous impulse, the true spirit of Christmas, remains with me, however imperfectly.

Michael Murtagh

Working with 'Gunnes'

I left school in Newry in 1974 during the first term of my 'A Levels'. I simply did not return after spending Christmas at home. My age was sixteen, coming on seventeen, as is said in those, 'want to be older' days. I had decided unilaterally that my future lay with my father in the family business and I consequently, without consultation with anyone, abandoned my studies. Nobody challenged the wisdom of my decision or offered an alternative option.

Each time I attend secondary schools and see the network of care which is now part of the school system, including year-heads, careers advisors, counsellors and chaplains, I am amazed at the resources and the interest invested in each pupil. I had attended boarding school for much of my own school time and while it was frugal it was not cruel. There was simply an absence of care. Each student, from the youngest of us at eleven years of age to the eighteen year old final year students were cut off from family and from the web of care which usually unites home, school and community nowadays. We were being formed in the disciplines of the monastery, in silence, study, independent living, cleanliness of self and environment, self-control and practice of religious duties. I could have been forgiven perhaps for wanting to escape from this routine but I did not have any real complaint at the time. Like most sixteen year olds, I just wanted to leave school. My motivation in all this had been to remain within a family tradition. The multiplicity of choices of career and the prospect of college or university was simply not considered. That was for another class of people.

A year after leaving school I took a part time job with an auctioneering firm (P.B. Gunne. Ltd) as a trainee livestock auctioneer. Like many jobs then, it was acquired by knowledge of someone who knew someone. My job initially was to act as clerk to the senior auctioneer in the livestock marts while I learnt the trade. Every mart day I set up the rostrum, with wooden gavel, to hammer out the deal, with microphone and with a large reel-to-reel tape recorder capable of eight hours recording. This was to record each sale so as to have a record available to settle disputes which arose in the evening. Late evenings and breaks for refreshment did funny things to farmers' minds and memories. I would take my place beside the auctioneer, in my white dairyman's coat and my job was to record owner, description of beast, weight, price, vendor and purchaser.

Weights, traditionally in the livestock industry were calculated in hundredweights, quarters and stones. The weight and the price offered or received had then to be calculated to a ratio of pounds per hundredweight for the farmer. This process became more complex when a European Union directive insisted on the use of kilograms and the weighbridge was changed to the metric measure. Kilograms then had to be mentally calculated back into hundredweights, quarters and stones and then into pounds per hundred-weight.

The mart itself was a relaxed mixture of roguery and dealing acumen. It was market forces at their worst and at their best. Competition meant that farmers frequently got the best possible prices, but ignorance of the system left the weak or unknowing to the mercilessness of the free market. Economic vultures hover everywhere the free market allows them. The farmers who frequented the place were often smallholders who appeared as though they had walked straight from the set of Kavanagh's 'Tarry Flynn' and the dealers, the, 'fair green gods' as the same Kavanagh called them had their own pride and etiquette. Their dress code often included the well known 'yellow boots', with a cane topped by a brass ferrule perhaps and a crombie overcoat if he was very important, or a navy dairyman's coat for the unpretentious. With the virtual disappearance of the small-holder and the trend towards agribusiness the way of life which the cattle mart epitomized seems to have had its day.

The dung and dirt of the cattle mart is to give way to a temple of modern living, an emporium of dealing of a different and more hygienic kind. Weights will still appear in kilos and the prices are in Euros, necessitating more mental conversion skills. The vets, 'department men' and dealers will have to take their business out of town, to wide open spaces, or perhaps take their product straight to the factory. The hurried song of the auctioneer will be replaced by 'musak' in the aisles.

Michael Murtagh

Minding the shop

The abuse of alcohol debate has been around for a long time now. It has been given a new and sharper focus in recent times because of the link with high profile crimes. I spent my formative late teens and early twenties working in my late father's pub. I left school at the age of sixteen to work with my father in the family business. He had recently inherited it from his bachelor cousin. Like many single people, our cousin had become set in his ways, unchallenged by those few who managed to get close to him. He had settled for the dozen good customers of like mind to himself that wisdom said was enough to keep a pub open, if not thriving. The business that was once a pub; grocer shop; drapery; coal and meal store and auctioneer's office had now shrivelled to the point where the only business left was that of the pub. My father had served his time there in the scarcity-soaked days of World War Two. He was apprenticed as a shop-boy to his uncle for three years at fifty shillings a year, payable to his father, brother to brother. The uncle died and my father later moved away, working as a barman in several places including Cootehill, Banbridge and in Crossmaglen, this time in a neighbouring business. He never spoke of the 'pub' but rather of the 'shop'. The old terminology of the pub cum grocery had not left him. He did not except to inherit his late uncle's place, where he had served his time, but on the invitation of his elderly and ailing cousin, my father's journey came full cycle, back to the counter where he had first served alcohol as a shop-boy. 'You never went to a barman's funeral' it was said. He was always a publican before he died.

My father and I set about renovating and updating the premises. The war rations of Fry's cocoa, packaged and tied up in brown paper and string, along with the dried, tinned 'Carnation' milk and triangular tins of 'Spam' corned beef were all thrown on the bonfire or on the trailer. The dividing wall between the bar and the now empty grocery was removed. The snugs and their confessional secrecy were demolished in favour of a more open-plan premises. The dividing walls that Victorian sensitivities had erected were coming down fast. The former drapery became the new lounge, complete with padded seats and red flock wallpaper. The yard toilet was moved inside and a bolt was provided on the back of the door so that an occasional lady could be catered for. The high, late Victorian counters were thrown out along with the shelves and mirrors and the greasy, under-counter money drawers. The oxtail-coloured exterior wood framing was removed and the black-out blinds that were more remnants of the Second World War were cleaned and restored. We installed a chipboard and Formica-topped counter. We tiled the wooden floor that had absorbed generations of spills and spits, and we faced or de-faced the shop-front with a bright plastic sign decorated with cocktail-glass trimmings, declaring the family name and announcing loudly the image makeover that we had just completed. The 'shop', with all its fussy detail and careful divisions, had moved into a new age, the age of the open, spacious lounge bar with all its garish decoration and kitsch ornaments.

The culture of drinking had moved on too. Women were welcomed in the lounge if not quite yet in the bar. They no longer had to wait for honourable old age to slip into the snug for their reward of a regular few bottles of milk stout. The variety of drinks and the technology of presenting them changed too. The 'half-one and bottle' brigade of farmers and returned navvies were eventually displaced by the affluent, advertisement-led, 'Bud' generation, drinking chilled lager from their long neck bottles. The Formica and chipboard didn't last the course and the Victoriana that had been abandoned in the hen-house as a roost began to make a comeback. The novelty and simplicity of the first feminine, mould-breaking drinks, Vodka and Pernod gave way to the multi-ingredient, pre-packed alco-pops of different shades that now make the back of the counter look more like a chemist shop than a pub. We have become European-ised too. We are beginning to see that there is more to wine than the sticky Sandemans port wine that beginner-drinkers, ladies, or men who were half keeping Lent used to indulge in.

My father maintained that the much maligned young people of his later years were more responsible in alcohol than his own contemporaries had been. His contemporaries, he maintained, didn't drink as much because they could not afford to do so, but when they indulged, on fair days or at markets, they were just as violent and aggressive and contrary, if not more so. They were more likely to drink and drive and more likely to deprive their wives and families of resources to the point of severe poverty and starvation.

Occasionally we are forcefully reminded of the the dark side of our culture of affluence and of alcohol. We cite the conviviality of the Irish as a part explanation for our love of congregating in pubs. There is some truth in that. Pubs provide company that is emotionally undemanding. They provide opportunities for meeting, for the cross-pollination of ideas and opinions. The disinhibiting effects of alcohol can make for a relaxation of tension and inspired repartee. The main reason, apart from the obvious climate-centered ones, for frequenting the pub too much rather than indulging in some other kind of leisure activity is cultural deprivation. Pubs and alcohol have inspired some great literature but it is the lack of leisure interests outside of television, tabloids and horses that drives many people to the counter or to the night club. The challenge of abuse of alcohol will never be fully or adequately dealt with by law or by education. Alcohol fills more than a gap in the stomach. That gap needs to be explored if we are to get to the root of the problem.

Noxious Weeds

In August 1971, around the time that internment without trial was introduced in Northern Ireland, my family decided to move off the land and into the village. My older brother and I moved into our new house first, as a kind of advance party. The rest of the family followed on in a few days. A new housing estate had been built and my mother had been appointed warden to the block of senior citizens' homes that were part of the estate. My father continued to work full time in the licensed trade and to farm the family land as a part-time activity. Living in the 'town' or in 'Cross' as we call it locally was a new experience for us. Another instalment of community and family drama began.

The introduction of internment was preceded by the shooting dead of a local man while he was working in Belfast. His vehicle backfired and he was shot dead by a nervous British soldier. In an unconnected development, internment was announced a day or so later. Amazingly, only one local man was interned. It was one too many and he was treated brutally during his imprisonment without trial. Southernmost Armagh remained relatively untouched, in terms of prisoners, by the sweep of internment. The death of the local man, however, coupled with the introduction of internment without trial sparked off an eruption of violence of volcanic proportions.

Pavement slabs were prised from their sandy foundations and broken into missile-sized pieces. Post-office vans, with their Royal Mail crests were taken from their storage depot and burned. Their shiny, post-box red bodies became, in turn, smouldering barricades, or later, rusty tin carcasses covering tell-tale scorch marks on the walls and on the tarmacadam. The local police barracks was one of a kind, built to a specification that made it immediately recognisable as a police building. Its defences were severely tested over the several nights of rioting that followed on the twin events of the Belfast murder and the introduction of internment.

The local police sergeant shared the same family name as me. He too, had recently moved into one of the larger of the new houses in the estate. His wife and two daughters were at home, a few doors away from me and my brother during those nights of rioting. I wondered if they, like us, initially regretted their recent decision to move house. My question was soon answered when a riotous gang attacked the policeman's house. He was absent, perhaps on duty in the barracks. His car was overturned and burned outside the house. His windows were broken and his wife and daughters cowered under the stairs, terrified. In my selfishness, I hoped that the rioters wouldn't attack the wrong house, given that our family names were the same. The sergeant and his family moved away shortly afterwards.

The police barracks developed into a military installation incorporating the old building. A perimeter wall was built and new accommodation and facilities for the military were added. Normal policing ceased and has never resumed. The only time we saw police for many years afterwards was while they were in the protection of a strong military presence. I had reason to go to the police station once, several years ago and I was amused to observe that the old wooden notice-board that used to hold police posters still stood inside the new perimeter wall. It leaned rather than stood. The wooden frame had sunk into the disturbed earth on one side giving it a decidedly lop-sided stance. The posters that had been last placed on it were still visible, though faded and dog-eared and obscured by the uncleaned, misty glass that protected them from the elements. The posters were mundane rather than dramatic. There were no urgent, 'Wanted' mug-shots of dangerous criminals or promises of riches and 'Reward'. The posters simply informed the local farming community that, under pain of fine, they were obliged to cut and destroy all ragweeds, thistles and other noxious weeds. The disturbance of the soil around the base of the notice board and the neglect that allowed it to fall into disuse and disrepair had provided the opportunity for a fine crop pf ragweeds and thistles, dockens and nettles to grow tall and strong, in blatant, incongruous disregard of the police notices.

The military installation continued to expand over the years, stealing and swallowing up neighbouring properties or part of them, most infamously taking over part of the playing field of Crossmaglen Rangers. An elderly couple lived next door. They kept a beautiful flower garden until their deaths and the compulsory acquisition of their property. Their bricks and mortar bungalow home and the very earth of their garden was carried away in a convoy of army lorries. I couldn't help noticing a solitary daffodil, in bloom and bending with the breeze, perched on the very top of one departing lorry load of top-soil and rubble. The military complex is a huge eyesore and irritant, still occupying the property of its neighbours. Huge, pylon-style, metal spikes pierce the sky. They carry cameras and electronic equipment, part of a countryside-wide complex of look-out posts. It is also a helicopter airport and the police and military centre for the area. The former R.U.C., now the re-named P.S.N.I. have not lived locally for decades. They still need a heavy military back-up and most of the force has no traditional sympathy with the area or with its people.

The reason I write down these memories and observation is to encourage you to reflect on the nature of our police force in the republic, the Garda Siochana and on your experience of them over the years. As the spotlight of public judgment sets on some members of the force, remember to keep a sense of proportion and of justice. Insist on high standards yet retain a keen sense of the reality of human imperfection. Remember also to judge those who judge and to assess the assessors. Disregard those for whose opinions you have no regard.

Michael Murtagh

Law & disorder

During the 1970s Crossmaglen and most of South Armagh was effectively a no-go area for the then police-force, the R.U.C. The British army patrolled the streets and kept the flag flying in this outpost of the empire but routine police presence was impossible without the protection of large numbers of back-up troops. In these conditions, law-breaking of a certain kind flourished. Cars were left untaxed. Tyres were left to go shiny or simply wore down to the wire. The publicans kept publicans' hours, opening and closing as they wished. There was little criminality of other kinds because of the internal threat of paramilitary punishment-squads but Government rules were fair game for the breaking, for getting around, over, under or through. The Irish have had, in their recent history, a healthy contempt for the laws of the colonizer.

Having tolerated this state of affairs for some time, the Northern Ireland Office decided to reclaim South Armagh to the rule of law. Their decision was partly prompted by some unwise posturing in the print-media which declared that the police would never walk the streets of the capital of Free South Armagh again. In due course the police returned in numbers. Cars were hastily taxed and shod again. Pub staff tried to persuade their after-hours customers that the police were really 'on the town'. I was one of the victims of this crackdown in that our pub was raided one night by the police, at eleven forty-five, fifteen minutes after closing time. I was helping my late father to get the customers out and I was holding a side-door open while some people were going out. My father and I were both fined for having people on the premises and for allowing them to drink. We were acquitted of a third charge of selling alcohol as there was no evidence that we were still serving customers. My fine was for 'aiding and abetting' my father's unlawfulness.

During this traumatic changeover to the rule of law a debate arose one day in our bar as to the desirability of having it imposed on us again. It was a typical bar-room debate with flashes of humour and wisdom, interspersed with the ridiculous and the improbable. It wasn't as if there was a choice either. The security forces had decided to re-take South Armagh in terms of law and policing. The days of no-go areas in Northern Ireland had passed. It was simply too embarrassing for the British Government. In the winding up of the bar-room debate on law and order, one heavyweight delivered the final verdict on the then current question as to the desirability of the return of normal policing.

He summed up the ambivalence of the Irish attitude to law when he pronounced from aloft his corner barstool that what we wanted in Crossmaglen was, 'order - but no law'.

This incident came to mind recently as I heard the stories that are currently being told of those publicans who are daring to openly break the (Irish) law on smoking in the workplace. I have to admit that I was astonished at the acquiescence of the Irish public when the law was brought in. We do not usually see ourselves as a law-keeping people. When most people think of Ireland it is not law that first comes to mind. We are not scrupulous law-keepers like some other cultures or like people from other traditions who share the island with us. I remember noting the relative elasticity of the law as it was applied to pub closing hours south of the border as against the cut-and-dried approach as applied on the northern side.

There is an antinomian streak in our history, an anti-law mentality that dies hard within us. This is encapsulated in the story about the Irishman who was shipwrecked and who survived. He clambered ashore the nearest island where he was greeted by a group of friendly natives. He replied to their greeting by declaring, 'Whatever government this place has - I'm agin' it'.

In the light of this perceived anti-law tendency, I have waited for stories to emerge of how individual publicans might interpret the law to the advantage of smokers or of how they would build by-passes around the legislation. I simply can't imagine country pub-goers on a winter's night sitting with unlit pipes cold in their pockets or sucking smokeless on their cork-tips because the government has decided that smoking in public houses is illegal.

The provision of shelters and outside facilities seems to be the furthest that pub-owners have gone to facilitate their smoking customers. This has given rise to the oddity of benches with sun-shades that have heaters built into them under the canopy being placed outside pubs for the convenience of those who have to nip out to light up. A fine line seems to be emerging between what is termed 'outside' and what is termed 'inside'. Anecdotal stories are told of how, in rural pubs, when the outsiders are gone, the ashtrays are taken out.

The introduction of a law that insists on clean air in the workplace is undoubtedly a good development. Perhaps its generous reception by the Irish public shows a growing maturity in our attitude to law. Attitudes change and laws evolve to reflect this. Health issues are at the top of any list of contemporary public concerns and public habits confirm this preoccupation. Maybe it is because the law is Irish-made and reflects Irish concerns that it has been received well by most. Those whom it has the potential to hurt financially, publicans and tobacco manufacturers, are the exception to the general rule.

The Irish have not always had a negative attitude to law. For centuries the set of laws that were known as the Brehon laws passed from oral tradition into written codes and they were generally well regarded as they were not considered foreign or restrictive. With the coming of various sets of invaders different sets of laws evolved and different ways of approaching law. This development inspired changing attitudes in the people who were subject to them. These laws were often conceived by foreign minds and enforced by foreign powers and they evoked a negative response in many cases. The Penal Codes of the late seventeenth century were the most notorious of these restrictive laws. The statesman Edmund Burke famously described this code of laws as, 'as well-fitted for the oppression, impoverishment and degradation of a people as ever proceeded from the perverted ingenuity of man' The legacy of these laws and the mentality that developed in response to them and by extension, to laws in general may finally be melting in the reception that has been given to an Irish law passed by an Irish parliament for the well-being of the Irish people, if not for harassed Irish publicans.

Michael Murtagh

Attacking the barracks

In 1976 my family was living in a housing estate in Crossmaglen. During those troubled times in Northern Ireland attacks were regularly made on military installations or there was the occasional 'attack on the barracks' as we put it. Such an event inevitably meant trouble for the townspeople and especially for young males. The soldiers would feel stung and they regularly behaved in a very aggressive and often dangerous manner. Some regiments built up especial reputations for brutality. On the last day of August 1976 the local barracks was attacked and the soldiers reacted in this predictable manner. Around twenty local men were arbitrarily arrested that evening.

Several of them later made statements that were recorded a few days later by the then Fr Denis Faul. He and Fr Ray Murray were documenting and publishing the unlawful killings of the time, the many civil rights abuses, the physical and the verbal abuse, some of which had sexual undercurrents or 'sexual humiliation' as it is now termed. The British Army knew that their misdemeanours were being monitored but they dismissed this work as 'propaganda for use in America'. I remember Fr Faul arriving in Crossmaglen to take such a statement. His initiative gave some hope to a battered and hope-less people. Who could one complain to? It was foolish to complain to the Army about the Army. The police appeared to be colluding with the violators and trust had never been strong in the police force anyway within nationalist communities. There was no political process with the ability to highlight these abuses and little hope of justice, but at least the abuses were being recorded. It seemed that someone cared.

The ill-treatment of Iraqi prisoners by American soldiers and by others with the subsequent images that have been shown all over the world have re-awakened memories in many Northerners who lived through the worst of the recent 'Troubles'. The killings, in suspicious circumstances, of children and of adults in Iran and elsewhere evoke a feeling of déjá-vu; of having seen this behaviour before and of having lived through it. There was no world-wide outcry at the time. There were no images of the abuse of detainees on prime-time television. There were no apologies or excuses of the 'a few bad apples' kind and few convictions. Only the folk memory of the community and the assiduous recording of Fr Faul and Fr Murray now testify to some of the terror of the time. One of these statements, recorded in 1976 following an outburst of such abuse by the Royal Marine Regiment reads as follows:

'On Tuesday evening, August 31 at 7.30 p.m. I heard shouting and screaming outside and I came to the sitting room window. One of the soldiers saw me at the window and he said: "Get that bastard in there." They pushed in the door and grabbed me and ran me to the Saracen (armoured car) and kicked me on the floor.

When we got to the barracks I was kicked from all directions by the soldiers. I was pulled out of the Saracen. In the yard I was put up against the wall in the search position, arms and legs outstretched. I got two belts of the butt of a rifle in the ribs and I was told to take off my jacket and empty the contents and open the belt of my trousers and take off my shoes.

I got a couple of thumps in the face from a man who said he was injured and I got about three kicks between the legs from behind. I fell on the ground and was told to get up again. I got a couple more kicks between the legs and I was asked were they sore enough.

We were told to run to the back of the barracks with our belongings. They made us run through the broken glass - we had no shoes on us and they made us stand up against the galvanise in the search position; one came to me and the man with me and asked us did we fancy a few rounds with him. He gave me a thump in the groin. Then we went by helicopter to Bessbrook. A soldier wanted to have a go at me with the butt of his rifle; he was told to sit down.

We were landed in Bessbrook; we had to run the gauntlet of the troops out of the helicopter at the landing place. We were lined up against the wall in a field and told to take our coats and shoes off again. One soldier allotted a civilian to each soldier. He said, "Run for the road." He twisted my arm above my shoulder, told me to make a run for it or he would break it. He ran me into the barracks in that position.

I was brought to the top of the yard and he put another fellow with blood on his face beside me. I was standing on a wooden pallet for a fork-lift. He told the other man to get on it as well. The pallet was 5 feet from the wall. I was told to get my feet to the outside of it and to each corner and stretch out my arms until my finger tips were touching the wall. The same for the man beside me. My left arm collapsed completely. I was told to move one piece of the timber and held myself up with one arm. I was there twenty minutes in that position when I fell. I was told to put my toes in between the timbers and get my arms up and sit in that position for twenty minutes - there was aching in my ankles. Another soldier came in and asked what was I doing in that position. He told me to get back into the more difficult position.

I could not get the left arm up. He said he would do it for me. Then he told everybody else to stand back from the wall and wriggle their fingers to get the circulation back, but to keep their noses to the wall. Two men had collapsed. I fell on the pallet and I was pulled over on to the yard and told to do press ups. I got my elbows on the ground and tried to raise myself, but my ankles failed. Another soldier hit me a kick and smashed my watch to pieces. He used sexually abusive language to me.

I was taken out to another compound. I was asked my name and religion. He told me I was an atheist. I was told to hold the blackboard with the details to be photographed. I could not hold it up and it was done for me. I was taken to a cell and given my belongings. After an hour I was taken out. I asked for a doctor - he noted my injuries, arms, legs, testicles and nose. I was interviewed by the Intelligence or Special Branch. They made no effort. The soldiers boasted of running Crossmaglen and I think the operation was an effort to terrorise us. After release I was in Craigavon Hospital for treatment. This was the first time I was "lifted" by the Army'.

It was also the last time. The door that was burst open and the house that was raided that evening was my family home and the statement above was made by my older brother who was then twenty years old.

Michael Murtagh

The way of the cross

Many years ago, long before I became a priest, I had the misfortune to be involved in a fatal road traffic accident. I fitted the profile of those most at risk of being involved. I was a young male driving a powerful car. Thankfully, the accident did not happen at night or where there was any question of alcohol having been consumed. It happened one morning in Belfast while I was returning from visiting a friend in hospital. The situation became difficult in that the accident happened in a Loyalist area of the city and I had to be spirited away by the police when my South Armagh address became known to the crowd that began to gather at the scene. I was later advised by the police not to contact the bereaved family of the person who had died. The prevailing tensions and troubles and the apparent paramilitary links of the bereaved family precluded any contact between us. In a court case about a year afterwards I was acquitted of any blame for the accident and subsequent death but it took me some time to acquit myself.

The experience of being the driver in such circumstance has left its mark on me. Many drivers are reckless and criminal in their behaviour but many others are simply caught up in road traffic accidents through no fault of their own. To this day I have a special concern for the drivers whom I come in contact with who have found themselves suddenly and innocently at the centre of an evolving tragedy. There is a deep human tendency to blame ourselves, to take on the burden of guilt, to accept fault. It may be appropriate to feel guilty, even shameful for wrongs committed but there is a guilt and shame which can be inappropriate and even self-centered in that it seeks to centre all fault on oneself as if the self was the cause and centre of all things. With these caveats and memories in place, and in the shadow of so many recent road traffic accidents, allow me to repeat a portion of something written for Viewpoint in 1999.

There is scarcely a mile of road on our major routes which is not inhabited by the shadows of our youthful dead and evocative of memories of life lost and lives scarred. Every bad corner, major junction, and memorial cross marks the spot where all things changed in an instant for some family and for some individuals. For those who remember, the most common of routes can become a Via Dolorosa, a way of the cross.

The cold statistics of road traffic death throw up their own pattern. These incidents happen most frequently to young adults, young males especially. They often involve a lethal cocktail of youth, speed, alcohol and carelessness or carefree-ness. The figures remain a reproach to those who believe that information or education alone can change behaviour. We do not easily learn from experience, especially when that experience hits our lives indirectly or at a tangent. Even the incomprehension and shock at the death of acquaintances and friends wears off and old habits are resumed. The invulnerability so keenly felt by youth, is not particular to youth. When the figures of road related deaths take on flesh, a legion of lost opportunity and wasted life and an army of bereaved and broken relatives is revealed. The figures for fatal road traffic accidents also remain a blackspot on the reputation of Co Louth.

There is a term, 'ludic suicide' which maintains that some like to play with death, to court death or live close to the edge at times. Playing with life and death as in Russian roulette or playing chicken with the traffic might be examples. The heightening of tension and the 'rush' associated with it are the reward. It may be conscious or otherwise in the case of our driving behaviour. Dicing with death, our own and others, whatever term we use and however we explain it, is part of the culture of youth and of the experience of everyone who has ever pressed the 'boot to the floor'.

Death on the roads is one of the major killers of our generation. We are fortunate to live in a time when widespread death of our young from war, famine or epidemic is only a memory. The slow trickle of road deaths replaces the haemorrhage of war or famine or epidemic. The loss is the same. Human tears and heartbreak carve long furrows on the faces of survivors. The dreaded knock on the door becomes a reality for the few and the night time vigil of most anxious parents continues. How we deal with death on our roads, or whether we deal with it remains problematic. 'Youth must have its fling', they say.
Meantime, death goes on.

Michael Murtagh

The 'troubles' come home

On a November night in 1974 the troubles in Northern Ireland really and literally came home to me. I was then a teenager studying at school for my 'A' Levels and helping my father occasionally in the family pub. Up to this point I had been somewhat sheltered from the troubles because I attended a boarding school. One of my father's sisters had died and we were preparing for the funeral. As is the tradition in family-run businesses in rural Ireland, we closed down the 'shop' for the duration of the wake and the funeral. We closed and bolted the tall double doors that faced the street and drew down the heavy black-out blinds that were a relic of World War Two. All that could be seen then was the outline of the oxtail-coloured shop front; the white script on the glass over the main entrance notifying the public that the proprietor was licensed to sell alcohol for six days a week and the wooden frames that held the bevelled glass notifying the public of what was available in their house; Wines, Spirits, Ales and Beers.

Laws and their application are invariably a little more elastic in borderland areas than elsewhere, even when the laws are self-imposed or made obligatory by social convention. The exception to the rule of the closed shop that night in North Street were the diggers of the family grave who had to be treated to drinks so as to satisfy the demands of common decency and it would be a bit daft to treat them elsewhere when we had a recently acquired pub of our own. My older brother was 'minding the shop' which with its blackout blinds appeared, from the outside, to be closed when what was thought to be a Loyalist gang struck just a few doors away. A neighbouring pub had a bomb placed outside it and a family home that had been carefully selected was attacked as the bombers fled. Two men were badly injured in the ensuing explosion. One of them, who happened to be outside the pub waiting in his taxi, survived terrible injuries. Another man who had been terribly injured, recovered somewhat at first, but died some months later.

The most enduring memory that I have from that night is that of sweeping up broken glass outside the family business. The pub windows had been glazed many decades beforehand with thick panes of glass and these had broken and fallen on to the footpaths like shattered ice that had slid from the slates in a thaw. The people inside were shocked and shaken but largely unharmed and unstirred. They were grateful that they had survived the blast and had not ended up as its direct targets. The thick, black blinds from the wartime black-out had contained the flying shards of glass and they had ended up in tatters, swinging loosely in places from the blown-open windows or showing their slash wounds as they were swept up on broad shovels from the outside paths, along with the glass and the debris. It was the first time but not the last that the pub windows would be blown in or sucked out by the force of explosives. The incident was very frightening because it was the first direct bomb attack on a pub in the town and it was the first local incident that was thought to be the work of Loyalists. It had been generally supposed that they were afraid to make sorties into the area until that night. The question remains as to whether the perpetrators had cover from the authorities. Nobody was ever convicted for the incident.

A different country

In 1975 I was seventeen years old. I was working full time with my father helping to run the family pub and small farm having left school the previous Christmas. The period just before Christmas was, as always, hectic. There were groups of workers in the pub marking the end of a season. There were those who only got drunk at Christmas and were therefore unpredictable in their intoxication, and there were the incessant calls for 'carry-outs' which meant searching for unusual items, wrapping bottles, and preparing a bill. This was sometimes followed by an argument about the cost, grounded on the dubious base of all the money the customer had spent with you that year.

In 1975, there had been some particularly nasty sectarian killings. Pubs were often an easy target for car bombs and for that reason we were trying to be vigilant. During the evening, despite the loud laughter and the din of well-oiled conversation, the muffled sound of an explosion was heard. Like the sound of thunder, we knew it was some short distance away and that it had come from a particular direction. Slowly, the word filtered back that it had been at the `Bridge, at Donnelly's pub, shop and petrol station a few miles away at

Silverbidge. As always, information came slowly and was clarified slowly. At one point a customer arrived into the pub carrying a driver's license. It was a standard issue Northern Ireland license, with an ink-blue hard cover and several inner pages. The predominant blue colour of this license had been overtaken by the scarlet staining of human blood, freshly shed, with which it was soaked. The license was opened and the photograph and identity details revealed the name of a local man known to all of us. His mother and mine were first cousins, which in country talk meant that we were 'friends', part of an extended family.

As the story unfolded, it became more tragic. My cousin, newly engaged, had also changed his car, and had gone to collect a new one. It was not ready and the filling stations at home were shut so he drove out to the neighbouring area of Silverbridge to fill up. The twelve year old son of the owner came out to fill the petrol. He and my cousin were gunned to death by a gang who also tossed a bomb into the pub. A group of workers from a nearby factory were celebrating the Christmas break-up. One was killed, several were terribly wounded.

As the news of the tragedy unfolded, someone decided to drive home my cousin's car, at which he had been shot. I remember washing the side and top of the car under the streetlight outside our home in Crossmaglen. With hindsight, it seems remarkable that such an important piece of forensic evidence should be removed from the scene. These were not normal times though. The police would not immediately respond to such emergency calls, for fear of being lured into an ambush, they would say. There were accusations later which suggested that the police, the U.D.R., or military intelligence, playing dirty tricks, may have been involved. Nobody was charged or prosecuted.

It is hard to believe that such were the conditions of those times. Sectarian massacres targeted areas rather than individuals. A spray of bullets and a tossed bomb in Silverbridge was fairly certain to kill a few Catholics, even if they were children and innocent bystanders. In the twisted thinking of the participants, it was three-nil, at least for that mission.

The families of the wounded and the dead learned to live again, in time, with the consequences of that random spray of death. They remained scarred, emotionally and physically and they have never forgotten the night their lives were utterly changed and they were caught in the deadly net of sectarian evil.

It has been said that the past is, 'a different country'. Remembering that particular night, it certainly seems so. At times I wonder if my memory is recalling accurately, so extraordinary were the times and conditions. We have become a different country over the past twenty-five years. We are a different people too. We are a sadder and a wiser people. Some things, however, remain unchanged. Truth and justice were and remain victims too, truth being traditionally the first victim of war. There remains a deep distrust of the security forces in the South Armagh area. What has changed is that the irresistible force of the drive for peace, an idea whose time had been long delayed, is now transforming life all over Ireland, but especially in areas which lived with the horror of sectarian attacks. Despite the shadow of unfinished business and the untold stories, despite the legacy of grief and the wounds of war, despite the brittle nature of the present peace, it is good to remember. Those who love, remember. They remember so that they may continue to allow suffering to purify and transform them, and so that those who do not remember and did not know the experience, may transform themselves and change society in a way which does not include gratuitous suffering and Christmas cruelty.

Following the Pope

In 1980, on September 14th, along with over seventy others, I entered Maynooth College to study for the priesthood. We were sometimes referred to as the class who 'followed the Pope into Maynooth'. It was not an analysis I liked as it made us seem unthinking and sheep-like. The effects of the Pope's visit were still strongly felt in the country and in the seminary then. Students imitated the Slavic accent of the Pope famously saying in Galway, 'Young people of Ireland, I love you'. Some, in high spirits, ritually kissed the ground on arrival at their destination, again after the example of the travelling Pope. There was even a feminist joke which ran, 'What's the difference between the Pope and Frank Sinatra? Answer: Frank Sinatra walks over the ground and kisses the women.

We were told, until it became a cliche that we were 'the future of the church'. New words like 'Popemobile' entered our vocabulary and folding chairs of the aluminium and canvas variety along with papal flags, umbrellas and yellow bunting were being stored away for the next time when the itinerary would include Northern Ireland. Less heard of or less repeated was the Pope's Drogheda plea, 'on my bended knees, I beg you to turn away from the path of violence...' Fifteen years were to elapse before a breakthrough and a ceasefire.

The event was, to those who lived in the latter part of the last century, what the Eucharistic Congress of 1932 was to those who lived in the first half, except this time it was the Pope, not merely a foreign Papal Legate. The visit brought its own cast of supporting personnel. Cardinal Tomás O Fiaich became a smiling household face. Bishop Eamon Casey and Fr Michael Cleary, added to their already substantial reputations as evangelical pastors and media personas. Archbishop Marcinkus did nothing to dispel his image as a heavy. Dana radiated the sweetness and wholesomeness which brought her to initial attention in the Eurovision. Journalists greeting the Pope, clapped and sang, 'For he's a jolly good fellow' at the Navan Road residence of the Papal Nuncio, Archbishop Alibrandi. A quarter of the total population gathered, like extras, at one venue alone when the Pope celebrated Mass in the Phoenix Park. These were dramatic days. There were personal stories of faith regained, of vocations, even of healing.

At the time, I was 'youth'. Well, I was twenty one and working, so I chose to go to Galway with a close friend of mine. Our visit was unremarkable. We made our way to Galway, to the racecourse at Ballybrit and we were assigned to a far flung 'corral' on the edge of the huge crowd as we belonged to no organised group. Most of the ceremony went over my head. I was more than a little distracted by the activities of the group directly in front of me who were sheltering from the occasional rain shower under a sheeting which covered a multitude. As far as I was concerned it was not a momentous or peak experience. It was more of a non-event for me.

On my way home, I stopped somewhere in County Cavan and bought a newspaper. In the inside front cover I read of the death of the parish priest at home. He was a traditional old man in his eighties. He died after a road accident, the final one of several in recent times. I knew him somewhat, my aunt being his housekeeper. We had several one-way conversations - he being quite deaf at this stage. He had sometimes suggested to my aunt that I might become a priest and she had relayed his comments to me later. At his funeral and afterwards, a sequence of thoughts, questions and reflections led me back to vocation, a consideration I had explored, deferred, rejected some times beforehand.

Several months later I sought an appointment with the new parish priest, had an interview with Cardinal O Fiaich in Armagh, and the following September arrived in Maynooth. Maybe I did follow the Pope into Maynooth, albeit by a circuitous route.

Ábhar Sagairt – The making of a priest

For the past few weeks I have been shadowed by Maynooth, past and present. The arrival of a current student of the diocese to discharge his 'pastoral placement' exercise prompted many questions about the current state of the place and retrieved a collection of lost memories and impressions that needed dusting down before they could be presented. Maynooth, for many clerical graduates tends to be a place that is easily forgotten. It might be more accurate to say that our memories of time spent there are quickly buried. There has rarely been a rush by clerical past pupils to return to the place. The student placement proved to be a mature, gifted, intelligent, well adjusted young man with a sense of humour and every need for it. He filled us in on the present structures, buildings and personnel, and the atmosphere or culture that prevails there.

I arrived in Maynooth seminary in 1980. I was twenty two years old. I had never seen the place before. The seminary is an old complex of buildings, gathered around a former gentleman's residence called Stoyte House. The college was founded in 1795. It was grant aided by the British Parliament until 1870. It was allowed and encouraged for pragmatic reasons. Priests were being trained on mainland Europe all through the Penal period and in the late 1780s it was believed that many were returning with what was called the 'French disease'- rebellious or republican tendencies. It was decided that it would be more pragmatic to train them at home where an eye could be kept on them and so the college was allowed, grant-aided and inspected regularly.

The complex of buildings that comprise the seminary carried some odd sounding names. My first address was Rhetoric House. That was a reference to the discipline of rhetoric that formed part of the training of a previous generation along with logic and grammar. I moved on to the appropriately named Long Corridor which was exactly what it said on the page, a featureless long corridor of rooms with numbers on the doors in a newer section of the complex. I later lived in Top Pat's, an address that continually confused my correspondents. I received letters in return addressed to me at Top Flats and Top Hats among other variations. The rooms were spartan and basic then. There was no central heating other than a single water pipe running through them. There was no hot water in the sinks and the electricity supply was limited so that heaters or kettles had to be used carefully. The accommodation was, as one early visitor to the college had described the dormitory in use then in Dickensian terms as, 'a do-the-boys-hall.'

I had spent some time at boarding school so the regime was not strange to me. I began to understand some of the customs that had been part of the boarding school culture and to notice that they had been transplanted from Maynooth. There was the same portrait gallery of gloomy former dignitaries along the high internal walls; the same terminology of deans, presidents, solemn silences and references to 'the house'. Maynooth had been carved into smaller replicas in diocesan junior seminaries and in boarding schools all over the country.

The course for seminarians began with the study of Philosophy, with metaphysics, the science of, 'being qua being', as we were told. We studied Communism in History of Philosophy along with ancient Greek philosophies and more contemporary movements such as existentialism. We also studied several obscure 'ologies' before moving on to the God stuff some years later when we studied Theology and all its component parts. The focus was academic. There was little or no pastoral training, no real preparation other than for exams. I still remember being shocked to discover that one of my soon to be ordained classmates did not understand how a cheque book worked. He was immediately appointed manager of a school, among other tasks, on his ordination some weeks later.

There was still a significant intake of students at the time and the body of student priests numbered several hundred. There was minimal supervision, partly because of the numbers and there was almost no personal attention. The National Seminary functioned as a priest-making machine squeezing out standardised diocesan priests, most destined for the trenches of the country's dioceses. Teaching standards were abysmal with one or two brilliant exceptions.

The place functioned as a tunnel, a necessary journey that impacted little on the individual other than holding out the promise of eventual release and the end of restrictions. Football helped to sublimate some of the natural energy and aggression. Top of the Pops was an equally obsessive part of the routine for many. Like most predominantly male institutions there was a good deal of aggression in the air and undercurrents of sexual energy that were never acknowledged. There were students who left because they had fallen in love with females with whom they had studied in the

National University campus. Some clerical students sneaked out for a drink occasionally or to socialise in the usual student manner. The greater part of any yearly intake would eventually leave, mostly after a few years when they had reached their early twenties and were clearer or more realistic about their lives. The atmosphere was generally adolescent. Little attention paid to the maturity of the student. Obedience and compliance were the paramount virtues whether or not the student had internalised the values he was proclaiming. There was negligence in many regards in that the place functioned, in my experience, merely as a large boarding school but there was no evidence of widespread or scandalous living. At least there was little that was obvious to the eyes of the average student. Life is complicated however and with the benefit of experience we began to read the signs a little differently and to understand the dark vein of pathology that ran through the place and that is no respecter of high intelligence, high office or holy intentions.

Michael Murtagh

'Movie' memories

Like many men I'm not very good at remembering personal anniversaries. In my case it doesn't matter too much. There's no one, not even myself, disappointed when I forget the anniversaries of the significant days in my life. Somebody reminded me today that it was the anniversary of my ordination to priesthood. I rarely remember the date. It has usually gone past several weeks when it comes, or is brought belatedly to my attention. The anniversary falls on the first day of June. The year it all happened was 1986. Some of my family were watching the video recently and reminiscing.

There were videos then - just about- and they were barely tolerated in churches. The video camera and operator were confined to an unobtrusive perch in the gallery. The angle was just perfect to pick up the bald pates and the thinning crowns of the gathered clergy and that of the twenty eight year old ordinand. In the week that followed there seemed to be a video just about everywhere I went. At one point I wondered if the rest of my life was going to be recorded on video. It's not a pleasant fantasy.

It's strange to have a walking, talking memento of those who have died since - to watch people walking and talking from beyond the grave. The video has the capacity to awaken memories that had been assumed to have gone forever like the cadences of voices that were once familiar and that have now been silenced by death. It can also reveal, in a way that is more heightened than in photography, the body language of people interacting. It's strange too to watch moving pictures of scenes and people that have altered radically in the intervening years. It's not that I watch the video too often. In fact I have only seen it once or twice in the years since. It's not pleasant to watch pictures of a drama in which you are one of the main participants. Vanity is a cruel judge and we do not like seeing ourselves as others see us habitually. It's the same for me with regard to wedding ceremonies. One of my nightmares is that of being asked to the home of the happy couple after the honeymoon is over to see the wedding video.

An ordination is a dramatic piece of liturgy. The man to be ordained is called forward from among his family and community to be ordained by the Bishop. He prostrates himself fully on the ground at one stage. His hands are solemnly anointed with Holy Oils for their sacred purposes. He is dressed in his priestly vestments, stole and chausible, having shed the crossed stole that is the sign of his former status as a deacon. The ordaining bishop and the priests present impose hands on his head in a gesture that suggests the calling down of the Holy Spirit. The ordained priest promises respect and obedience to his bishop and his successors. He is welcomed into the fraternity with the sign of peace, given in the form of an embrace, however awkwardly this may have been executed, by the priests of the diocese.

There then followed the usual round of 'first' Masses and public blessings. I remember the waves of people at the First Blessing. I also remember the muscles at the back of my legs becoming sore from the standing and moving sideways, like a crab, along the altar rails. When the celebration died down there was an intervening six weeks or so before appointment, the 'honeymoon without the honey' as one wit put it to me.

The video is an interesting resource for social history. Even within twenty years, so much has changed. The immediately obvious is of course the change that has taken place in people. Hair has gone grey or just gone. Styles that appeared so trendy and fashionable at the time now look corny. The social and the clerical atmosphere have changed too. In some ways the ceasefire of the last several years has taken the edge off the charged situation that was Crossmaglen in 1986. I still remember the bewilderment on the faces of the British Army when marching bands appeared to escort me the short distance from my home in North Street to the parish church to celebrate 'First Mass' on the Monday evening. This was a new situation for which they had no precedent or cultural parallel.

The strangest thing of all is, of course, the choices that the actors in this moving picture have taken in the intervening years and the destinies of some of the principal characters. No one could write the script that would have prophesied the unfolding story of the seventeen years since. The source of priestly vocations has all but totally dried up in the meantime in this end of the world and the video-recorded ceremony of ordination has become, for many communities, an historical memory, a visual, walking, talking record of how things used to be on the day that the priesthood was conferred, with much celebration, on a native of the parish and gladly accepted by significant numbers of young men who promised respect and obedience to their bishops.

Delayed Adolescence

During the week I had a chance encounter with someone I knew from seminary days, almost twenty years ago now. He had been attending Mass with a relative and thought that he recognised the priest-celebrant. He wasn't too sure at first, as twenty years does strange things to all of us. My friend had been one of a lively group who were slightly junior to me in the seminary and a few years younger than me, they having entered straight from college. They were having their student, late teens times of their lives and I was having my twenty-something delayed adolescence.

My friend made a point of calling to my house. I recognised him after only a moment of hesitation. Time has been kinder to him. In the thirty minutes available to us, we covered a lot of years and a lot of ground. We checked out the present whereabouts, where known, of past friends and their family and career developments. Most left the seminary as students and a significant number have left later on as priests. Eventually we moved on to our own situations.

My friend saved me some possible embarrassment by assuring me that he was still a priest. He knew that I would surely have heard the rumours of his leaving. He had taken 'time out'. The phrase is usually a euphemism for leaving, or a way of leaving with a soft landing. Not having the time and perhaps lacking the motivation to enter this difficult area, we did not explore the reasons why he had almost left or more importantly, the reasons he had decided to stay. I'm sure most priests and most married people have negotiated this terrain. The only difference is that my friend's decision making somehow left the realm of the private and surfed the choppy sea of rumour for a while.

My friend seemed content and had not lost any of his good humour, his charm or his abundance of human giftedness. We compared our personal situations and circumstances and moved on to the wider picture. We spoke of emptying seminaries and of the perceived personnel crisis in both our dioceses. We agreed that there was as yet no great need, only a dearth of good management. We deplored insipid leadership (in others of course) and we looked back wistfully and with amused detachment on the days of our training. Boy, were we raised innocent, ran the subtext.

It seemed to me that my friend had re-negotiated his vocation to priesthood, as so many others have undoubtedly done in the upheaval of the past ten years. Most decided to stay, some lacking the courage to leave the comfort of the nest, others deciding to stay for better reasons, better and more mature reasons perhaps than those which brought them into seminary in the first instance. Priests are staying in ministry increasingly on their own terms though. This is not an encouraging development.

There seemed to me to be a mood of detached commitment, a sense of waiting for better days which might or might not come in our time. There was a sense that present structures should be allowed to die rather than be temporarily propped up by the unstable. We both had a sense of survival against the odds and of living in strange, in-between times. Our shared student past was looked back on with incredulity because of the innocence and the incompetence.

Could any of us ever have dreamed that ordination would have led us into such confusing and troubled times? Hardly. Can we dream or envision our way into better times? Possibly.

Massabielle 1990

In May 1990 people were preparing for the annual pilgrimage to Lourdes as usual. A well oiled organisation was gathering the sick and pilgrims together and workers were looking forward to meeting their counterparts from all over the country at the five day stay in France. There was nothing unusual planned or expected.

Cardinal Ó Fiaich had been on his Confirmation circuit, busier than usual because of the death of his auxiliary, Bishop Lennon the previous October, from a sudden heart attack. He had also been busy collecting local lore on the Irish civil war from the few survivors left. Lourdes was part of his annual schedule and part of the appeal of the trip for pilgrims was the chance to meet and greet him there. His participation in the social life of the pilgrimage had come to be appreciated and well known.

On the morning of the first full day, Mass was at Massabielle, the rock grotto where the Virgin had appeared to Bernadette. The concelebrating priests gathered in the sacristy, dressed for Mass and awaited the appearance of the chief celebrant, the Cardinal. He arrived with little time to spare and greeted us in a subdued manner. He seemed tired and in the brighter light of the exterior, the pallor of his face was seen to be an unhealthy grey-blue. When he began to speak, it became obvious to those listening that the words were breaking in his mouth. To those of medical expertise the signs were ominous. Immediately after the Mass, he was examined, and whisked off to Toulouse by helicopter. I asked the late Dr. Frank O Reilly how ill the Cardinal was and he said that he had a 50/50 chance of survival.

In medical terms 50/50 seemed optimistic to me. I was obviously seeing only one half of the equation. The day wore on following the intended schedule and it was evening before reports of the Cardinal's death in Toulouse reached pilgrims. The news seemed impossible to believe. Within seven months, both bishops of the diocese were dead. It was decided to carry on with the pilgrimage, however unmotivated we might be, and as the logistics of returning so many people to Ireland immediately were impossible.

As the news broke, media people descended on the Pyrenean mountain town. The stage was set for a drama which lasted for some days. The Cardinal, though known for his affability did not enjoy universal good relations with the media. He had made some early mistakes and had become wary of the intentions of some journalists. The line taken by the descending journalists was that this was a good and decent man but a republican. The only subject they seemed to wish to explore was his relationship with republican politics. Tension soon heightened between the clergy, who were sought out as spokesmen, and the arriving reporters.

Over the next few days there developed a tense irritated communication. Occasionally it spilled over into mutual contempt. Relations were not helped by the lack of sensitivity to the deep feelings of shock and bereavement people were feeling. A female reporter from the Gerry Ryan show showed an appalling lack of taste by seeking out the tackiest Lourdes souvenirs and proceeding to lampoon them. A reporter I spoke to described the bishops at a requiem Mass as, 'those fellows with the cornflakes boxes on their heads'. He was juvenile in his boasting of how long he had been away from the church and the sacraments, and one nationally known journalist had to be stopped from physically attacking a priest whom he felt had been overbearing with him. He was prevented by his colleagues. He had identified the wrong priest and was not in a state of good judgement.

I am told that the mood of reporting changed in Ireland as it became obvious that national feeling did not match the prejudices of national media. The Cardinal had managed to become a household name, partly because of his exposure at the Pope's visit in 1979 and partly by force of his own personality and scholarship. He was an excellent communicator, especially with a group. In what had been tough times, especially in the North, he had shown solidarity with his people and given them a sense of pride in their history and in their identity. His likeness, uniquely, is still found in countless display cabinets in houses wherever I visit. No other church personality enjoys such uncritical acclaim. His cause was surely helped by the apparent efforts of the British to blacklist him in the Vatican.

The intervening years have seen a lot of developments. For the church it has been a dark night of the soul. The new millennium promises no easy solutions or imminent improvements. Media/church relations have changed little. The pilgrimage begun in May 1980 has become part of a longer pilgrimage into the great unknown.

Married to the church

I was walking with a friend through a busy main street recently when my friend called my attention to a voice that was trying to make contact with me. I had not heard my name being called. The noise of the traffic and the hum of commerce and of conversation on a crowded street had smothered his call of recognition. When the man came forward to greet me, he called me by the name that most clergy and former seminary colleagues would use for me - Mick. I hesitated for a minute but as soon as he began to speak again I recognised the unusual accent that had been his trademark. He had changed in appearance only to the extent that he had broadened and put on some weight. We quickly caught up with where he was living and working and who he was in regular contact with from the old days. He told me excitedly that he had written a book, had fathered a child and that his wife was expecting another. He wanted me to meet his wife but he wasn't sure what shop she had gone into. He had left the priesthood to be with her some few years ago. She had been in a failed marriage relationship, apparently and they had met in that context. He was waiting for her outside a supermarket when he spotted me in the street. I was glad that he had recognised me.

He had been a fellow student in the seminary. He had been ordained a priest and had served in his home diocese and in the developing world. He had been a good sportsman and he had a keen intellect and a love of literature. He was also a character. He was, to use the observation of one of our friends back then, 'cool as a breeze'. He skipped lectures, flunked exams, stayed out late, partied and slept late in the mornings and got away with it all. He came to my ordination in Crossmaglen and stayed for about a fortnight, almost forgetting to go home for his own. He was funny even without speaking. I recall attending a wedding at which he also was a guest, seated at the top table. He was invited to speak and he made his way to the microphone which was behind the bride and groom. The guests at the wedding were laughing even before he lifted the microphone. He had that gift that some comedians have of being able to move audiences to laughter without words.

I had to keep going on so we arranged that he would contact me and send me a copy of his work. This chance encounter with a colleague from the past led me to thinking of other colleagues in our group and of the stories that their lives have generated. When seventy five of us made our way to Maynooth in September

1980, the afterglow of the Pope's visit to Ireland was still warm. The life stories that we had dreamed up for ourselves and for our futures turned out to be so far removed from the real-life stories that unfolded and that continue to develop. What a story our collective stories might make.

An American had already thought of the idea and I had read his book some years ago. His name is Raymond Hedin and his book is called, somewhat curiously I thought, Married to the Church. He had left the seminary before ordination. He interviewed all of his class fellows from the year they had entered, whether they had stayed or left before or after ordination. He discovered that there were many shared observations about seminary life among the group. He recorded the general judgements about being too sheltered before entering the seminary and about the lack of maturity or opportunities for growth in the seminary training. He then went on to develop the traditional metaphor of being married to the church from which he took the title of his book. He wrote of the seminary days as days of courtship, a showing of the best side, times marked by company, warmth and support. He developed the analogy by describing the heady, celebratory days of commitment and the difficulties, the disillusionment and the gritty realities that come to light during the workaday routine that follows the honeymoon period. He described the dynamics of staying or going as having parallels with marriage and decided that priests know much more about marriage than they are generally given credit for.

Job description

Another week in the life of a country curate finished. Monday morning chores cast shadows over the few hours' relaxation that is grabbed following Sunday's frenetic round of Masses and Baptisms. My afternoon rest is broken by word of one of the several tragedies that accompany the celebration of a weekend in our drink-soaked culture. There is word of sickness too. There is the young man suffering from mental illness. There are the accompanying fears of his brave and struggling father and mother. There is the grandmother over whose life the shadow of imminent death has suddenly fallen. There is also the news of yet another priest who has collapsed under the strain of working too hard for too long.

There are the bright spots and the good memories of the week to look back on too. There is the exuberant joy of a class of seventeen year olds singing John Lennon songs as they celebrated their graduation from secondary school. There is the baptism of the strong and healthy child whose life hung in the balance just a few weeks ago. There is the wedding of the couple who have worked hard to secure their future and who now celebrate in what has become the traditional way with their extended families and friends. There is the wonderful innocence of the First Communicants who go through their paces to the rapt attention of their relations and teachers before counting the proceeds of their personal collections and going on the shopping spree that has become an unofficial part of the deal.

In all of these situations there is the unchanging role of the pastor looking after his people, the shepherd pasturing his sheep. There are many different roles to be fulfilled, some more obvious and some more onerous than others. The way they are fulfilled or not fulfilled depends on the way the pastor sees his people, whether, in his outlook, the people exist to serve his needs or he to serve their spiritual needs. The demands, from above or from below, according to the model of hierarchy, can be unrealistic at times. The satisfaction, when things are well, and our privileged access to people's lives can be rewarding too.

At its most primitive there is the demand for the priest in the role of magician or fixer. There is the expectation deep in the mind of some that somehow the priest can change things, can make things well again. The appeal of magical solutions is sometimes as strong in the devout as it can be in the irreligious. How many people can pass the horoscope page by when they are browsing the paper but feel compelled to look at it even though it has been persistently wrong over a lifetime? I confess to reading it sometimes myself just to smile at he predictions for my love life and for my financial future. We all need the dream appeal of magic solutions sometimes.

There is the related role of intercessor in which the priest is often cast. Many people approach the priest for prayers, believing that the prayers and the prayer life of the priest is somehow privileged. It is a role to be taken very seriously by the priest despite the misgivings he may have or the deficiencies he may feel. It is a role that is played out too when the priest articulates the concerns of the community in the communal prayers or prayers of the faithful that are said on Sundays or at weekday Mass. The priest is called too to interpret life for the community, to be something of a philosopher working out the great questions of life and suffering and death. He has to answer the great questions of his own vocation too, what his role is and why he is or remains a priest.

There is also the role in which some people would like to cast the priest as social judge and public agent of condemnation. There is a tendency in some people to relish public condemnation of persons or trends. The snag is that it has to be others and their sins that are to be condemned. There is a nostalgia for the old style certainties and the preaching that was tinged by hell fire. Whatever about the anaemic quality of much of our homilies now, there is no going back to the days of judgement. Too much has happened in the meantime to make such a return credible.

Along the way through the average week there are also the roles of the priest as liturgist, celebrating the rites of the church for and with his people. He may be occasional spokesperson for the community at public events. The priest is often called on for the 'few words' as spokesperson for the family at weddings and anniversaries. He has to be a counsellor and confessor, maybe not in the sacramental sense always, but carrying the burden of some of the secret sins of the community nonetheless. He may also be called on as arbitrator, as wise counsel and as the outsider who is beyond the blood and kin ties of a community and therefore not open to the same influence or bias.

There is the role too of the priest as motivator, the one who comes up with the ideas, harnesses the energy and talents of the community and gets the projects off the ground. He is expected too to be manager and fund-raiser. The priest may also take on other subsidiary roles such as the chronicler of community events, the local historian, the archivist and the custodian of the story of a community. He may be saddled with the job of being social worker, resource person, teacher, prophet and manager of property and funds. There are those church personnel too who invest themselves in buildings, working out what the Americans call their unresolved 'edifice' complex.

All of these roles and more too can crop up in the week of an active pastoral priest in Ireland. There was a time when no priest doubted that he would be replaced in the community when his time was up and he moved on. His role was secure and the worth of his life was beyond question. The background music was different then. The scenery was different, greener, at least in retrospect. The role was more defined and more valued in a general sense. As the weeks become months, the months become years and the years shape the future the only thing certain about the future of priestly life is that it will be different.

Michael Murtagh

Beginning with dessert

One of the phrases occasionally trotted out by observers is that there is a great, 'spiritual hunger' out there. I have often thought that this observation is little more than wishful thinking or an exercise in self-deception. It is a cliché that slips off the tongue rather too easily, a pious hope for some that religion of the traditional variety *'hasn't gone away you know'*. It sometimes cloaks a paternalist hope that the ungrateful lapsed will eventually make their prodigal way back to the church that reared them. The hunger that is more often seen is a hunger of the belly kind, a hunger for the pleasures and treasures of life, even a blatant greed for the more tangible, for entertainment, pleasure, material wealth and for social recognition or prestige.

Those who might be said to be searching hungrily for something less tangible more often head for alternative street, for the bright bazaars of the New Age, enjoying the exotic and revelling in the delight of being different. The mother's milk of mainstream religion is largely passed over. The traditional crock of spiritual gold remains hidden to them because they are not prepared to journey to rainbow's end. The false coin of a quick emotional fix is more immediately gratifying. Feeling good about oneself is the goal of much of this 'spirituality'. Feeling bad about oneself, at least when that's appropriate, and doing something about it; the traditional stuff of religion, is bypassed and vilified. Guilt or shame are sectioned, shut away and condemned as neurotic.

Some who like to keep a foot in both camps take an essentially lazy option and claim to be spiritual but not religious, not tied down by religious dogma which might force them to define what they believe and why. To accept the label religious might invite a raft of synonyms, religious taken to mean conservative, illiberal, superstitious or irrational. Those who claim a spirituality of this brand may feel that their lives are incomplete until they have added the spiritual dimension to their image, until they can sport the designer label of a fashionable trend. Some become angel-spotters, others aspire to be peace-loving Buddhists or transcendental meditators, anything that does not require doctrine, discipline, and devotion to somebody or something over and above themselves or, God forbid, sacrifice. They are hungry but they want to begin with dessert.

My mind has been somewhat altered regarding spiritual hunger by the visit of a friend. He was suffering from a hunger of some kind, a hunger he felt only religion might satisfy. He has all the trappings, a good, beautiful and devoted wife, a prosperous professional career, a house enjoying the triple delights of the estate agent, location, location and location, a car with a prestige badge and the pigeon's clutch; two healthy children. Recently his feelings of emptiness motivated him to give some of his time to charity work. He prays daily, goes to mass and is conventional in his lifestyle yet having achieved most of that which people commonly aspire to, he remains dissatisfied with life. A puzzled frown had descended on him. He is hungry for answers to basic questions. Despite his intelligence and education in the catholic school system he remains embarrassingly weak on basic religious knowledge. His life and his family have been largely untouched by death or tragedy, but the suicide of a close student friend had been and remains unsettling to him. One spiritual appetite hardly constitutes a great hunger yet the predicament of my friend seemed to provide some evidence of the spiritual hunger I had been hearing about.

I found it heartening too to deal not with hostility or evidence of corruption or worse still, with apathy but with honest constructive questioning, asking the right questions and searching in the right places. It was also pleasant that the questions did not arise from one of life's knockout blows but from simple reflection on the purpose of all the acquisition and prestige seeking of life. Asking fundamental questions had not led him to fundamentalism or easy answers. The Promised Land is not reached without a long weary trek through the desert.

Michael Murtagh

Bachelor boys

Aside from being damned by faint praise of the 'yis are not all bad' kind, one of the things I'm sure to be asked about when I am cornered at a public function is whether I believe that celibacy is a good thing or whether priests should be allowed to get married. The question is so complex that doing justice to it by way of an answer is difficult, even when I know that time is not my enemy. The kind of answer that is expected is the usual tabloid simplification of what is a complex human experience or phenomenon so I say that priesthood with its celibacy has generally been kind to me and maybe some day the rules will change to admit more exceptions to the rule of celibacy – but don't hold your breath. There are already exceptions made for former Anglican clergy who are married and for other groups that remain under the Roman umbrella like the Coptic Church which has its own rite for worship and its own rules for clergy. The principle has been conceded. Celibacy is not always inextricably linked with catholic priesthood. It has not always been enshrined in law either but it has always been part of the wider tradition. Some people see it as a 'waste' but it is precisely in the paradox of apparent waste that its symbolic power lies.

Questions about celibacy are almost exclusively asked of males. People forget that there are many more women living celibacy than there are males. The number of nuns who have taken on and have lived lives of celibacy has, for the past century or more, been several times that of the number of men. When is the last time you heard a nun being asked how she was coping with celibacy or if she thought nuns should be allowed to get married? The female experience of celibacy is almost always ignored, just as the male experience is almost always expected to be troubled. Marriage or freedom to marry is almost always given as a glib answer to all priestly problems. It is as if there was no violence within marriage, no sexual aberrations among those who are married, no addictions, or no lack of maturity among those who tie the knot.

There is also the assumption that because I am committed to celibacy and priesthood that I have been such since birth. I was what was then termed a 'late vocation' at twenty two years of age when I entered seminary to explore priesthood and to consider celibacy. I was twenty eight when I was ordained. These were the hardly rushed decisions of the inexperienced. There are few people so privileged as to have entered marriage with such opportunities of reflection on their vocational path or on the partner in life whom they had chosen. I had almost six years of freedom and adult living between leaving school and entering seminary and another six years of study, travel and thought before ordination. I can hardly be said to have had celibacy imposed on me yet that is what many people believe and hold to be true about celibacy in general.

A quasi-celibate life is lived by many people who are not priests or religious but who remain single and chaste, sometimes for life, out of religious conviction. Many people are celibate or chaste for long periods in their lives without adverse damage. The received wisdom in our over-sexualised, therapeutic society is that abstinence from physical expression of one's sexuality is a sure road to repression and subsequent eruptions or powerful explosions of a neurotic nature – what psychology calls the 'hydraulic' effect. Anyone not participating in the permissive society is suspect. My own experience has been that while I miss the unfulfilled physical side of sexual life and the prospect of spouse and children, I relish the freedom that celibacy gives and the opportunities it allows for the putting into effect of its true rationale – the development of the spirit and the total availability for service. Where maturity of character, integration of the personality, genuine spiritual development, availability to serve and simplicity of lifestyle are not present then it is bachelorhood or spinsterhood, not celibacy that is being lived.

There is no doubt that celibacy that is badly prepared for and poorly lived has caused problems. There were many candidates, particularly in the past, who were too young, too sheltered from life experiences or too immature to have taken such far-reaching life decisions. Even among the late vocations or 'mature' students that are more common at present, maturity of character cannot be assumed. Age or experience does not mean that a person has learned from either. There has always been the tendency for the celibate, unchallenged by wife or family, to slip into bachelor habits and selfish, rigid ways. In controlling their sexuality, some become over-controlled and over-controlling and lose much of their humanity in the process. I'm not sure that marriage, 'enforced' or otherwise, is the answer or the best option for them. As someone once remarked on observing a group of celibate priests, 'It's mothers they need, not wives'.

Michael Murtagh

Negotiating the shadows

Over the past fortnight or so I believe I have developed a little more insight into what it must feel to be a Muslim living in Western society at the present. As I watched an Irish gypsy woman being ejected (justly) from a family celebration in a hotel, I momentarily felt a heightened empathy with her too. The shadow of suspicion that has fallen over priests in the wake of the many revelations of the last decade has significantly darkened lately. As a Muslim must feel the suspicion of the western world piercing or as a gypsy must feel the negativity attached to their clan as a black cloud overhead, so I negotiated my way through the turbulence of the past two weeks anxiously searching the eyes of strangers and of friends for signs of condemnation or of acceptance.

I travelled collar-less most of the time. The prestige of this outward symbol of office has become a negative prestige. I attached a stock and collar under my jacket only when entering hospital or on very formal duties and removed it as soon as I returned to the car. I do this almost unthinkingly in the past few years. I was glad not to be wearing it when I walked through a newsagent's shop that had several rows of screaming headlines illustrated by photos of rogue priests and their innocent victims.

Leisure time is similarly mined with moments of anxiety. If a child wanders into my path while I am swimming and I touch that child, how might that be interpreted? If I find myself in the dressing room and a child wanders in, what ought I to do – react and remove myself or carry on. Moments of silence or aloneness take on the form of inventories of the past. Could anything I did in the past be misconstrued? Did I give money to anyone at the door or allow anyone to stay in the spare room? How might I react if a false accusation were brought? Liturgical moments are not anxiety free either. Do I sit down beside the servers as we wait for the time bell? Do I risk further suspicion by engaging them in banter or do I ignore them and keep a physical distance? These everyday, unstated dilemmas are played out in sacristies all over the country and farther afield. How do I face a class of searching teenagers with no answers to their questions about the absence of justice or of charity in the playing out of the abuse saga. There are a few, long involved discussions with priest colleagues, in person and by telephone. These are saturated by common feelings of shame, anger, futility and powerlessness, the very same feelings that many of our congregations share. As the late Cardinal Konig, former Archbishop of Vienna wrote some years ago, 'In turbulent times like these… the network of families and parishes needs information, communication, reinforcement, encouragement from the larger structures of the church which must be supportive and not dictatorial'.

It appears that at the core of the crisis is a number of priests (abusers in many categories) who have been, and some who still are, allowed to run amok. The church structures that existed only to serve God and God's people have periodically functioned or their malfunctioned as if mission was simply and only self-preservation and self-defence. Interested only in its own, corrupted by an unjudging tribal loyalty, unwilling to let one of its own down, the dysfunctional family tried to hide its secrets and its deficiencies from the world at the expense of violating the trust on which it survived. Stripped of all its theory, law and rhetoric, an attitude to people emerged that has been shown to be much less than worthy, and especially unworthy of preachers of the gospel of Christ. Priests, I believe, generally feel powerless to change anything, anxious about the present and the future, and neglected in terms of pastoral care by all but the few lay people who have the strength to encourage them, to reassure them.

Forty years ago, the fundamentals of all these problems were taken out from under the dusty Vatican carpet to be aired in the open window of the Vatican Council. This was an extraordinary event called by an extraordinary man, 'Good Pope John'. He won many admirers because of his humanity, his humour, his courage and his warmth of personality. He was an eternal optimist too. His opening speech to the council on October 11 1962 contained the following pertinent words:

'In the daily exercise our pastoral office, we sometimes have to listen, much to our regret, to voices of persons who, though burning with zeal, are not endowed with too much sense of discretion or measure. In these modern times they can see nothing but prevarication and ruin. They say that our era, in comparison with past eras, is getting worse, and they behave as though they had learned nothing from history, which is, nonetheless, the teacher of life. We feel we must disagree with those prophets of gloom, who are always forecasting disaster, as though the end of the world were at hand.'

Let's hope that history, the great teacher of life, finds keen students.

Michael Murtagh

Death of a mystique

Another investigative television programme. Another series of allegations and revelations. Another in a shower of apologies. Just when you think that morale cannot possibly take another battering, cannot possibly sink lower – it does. Why, some ask do you remain a priest in the face of such corruption and incompetence. The choice of priesthood as a way of life seems incomprehensible to many people at the best of times. I have been asked if it was 'for the money' that I joined the ranks of the priesthood. I have also been asked whether it was because of sexual orientation or whether I was forced in some way to enter the ranks of the clergy.

There are few lifestyles that evoke more interest and wonder than religious vocation and celibate commitment. There was, especially in past decades, a mystique that surrounded the 'call' and the commitment to celibacy that followed. There was also the aura of mystique that surrounded those who lived out that call especially when they held high office. The aura or mystique that attached to religious was the origin or seed bed of many stories, many suppositions and a great many misconceptions. The truth that the daily struggle with commitment and the testing life of a vowed religious or priest was as difficult as it sometimes is, was not generally admitted. Clergy often colluded in painting a rose-tinted picture. Clergy leaders often worked out of a model of priesthood or religious life that was largely mythical or imaginary or impossibly and implausibly pious.

Some of what we are seeing at the moment is the death of that mystique. It is not often that we have the privilege of witnessing such a demise. The constant revelation of the sordid in the life of some troubled clergy and the public revealing of the blatant self-interest of those who failed to deal adequately with them are signs of the death of a mystique, an aura that once enveloped and protected the clergy and others, especially those who held office and consequent power.

There is always the comfort, whatever the storm outside or inside, of remaining in the nest. There is comfort in the familiar. There is the temptation to remain, to nest, because that is the most comfortable thing to do. The average middle-aged cleric would be traumatised to leave his familiar role, to abandon his well-trodden ways of life, to be thrown out of the nest, out of the spotlight, however local, into the uncertainty of the rest of his life. The adaptation needed to survive in a competitive, demanding, professional work environment would be huge. The demands of adjusting to the daily negotiations that are part of a mature intimate relationship would be very threatening for most of those formed in the solitary ways of celibacy.

There are other more noble reasons of course for not jumping ship, for not abandoning one's chosen way of life or vocation. There are promises made before God and witnessed by the community. There is work to be done and people's needs to be served. There is a ministry that is particular to most pastors, a charism or gift that is very individual. There is witness to be given to the possibility and to the reality of a wholesome, mature, integrated life as a priest or religious. There is service to be done to the people to whom you have been sent; to those to whom you are committed. There is the personal conviction that the one whose call you answered and who continues to sustain you will not abandon you.

There is also the hope that the future will be different. The immediate future promises only difficulties. There are tribunals and enquiries to report in the future and their findings will keep the public eye firmly on scandal. The exercise of authority and leadership and the use or abuse of power will remain under scrutiny. The personnel situation remains bleak. The seepage of ordained clergy out of ministry has become a leakage. There are only six students studying for the diocese at the moment. None at all have entered over the past several years. Increasingly fewer young people contemplate the possibility of working and living under the personnel management, the conditions or the outmoded and antiquated structures that regulate the clergy. The age profile of serving clergy is increasingly top heavy.

Those clergy who feel a deeper need to be hopeful or optimistic than to be realistic speak of light in the darkness, spring shoots below the frozen soil and purification after the fire. Those who are by disposition permanently defensive deny the evidence of decline and minimise the extent of the crisis. Some blame the rigidity and inadequacies of the old ways. Others blame the blast of modernity that hit the church forty years age in the wake of the Second Vatican Council. Most simply carry on with their daily lives with the gritty reality of routine and of chores. They are sustained by their faith and by their prayers and by the encouragement and the generosity of spirit of the people they serve. They leave the future to those who will inhabit it, investing all their energy in the will to survive, in the struggle to continue and to remain healthy. They leave visioning the future to others. The view of the confused present seems enough to contemplate just now.

The Chinese are said to have a saying that reads, 'may you live in interesting times'. It is not a wish or a blessing but a curse. Interesting times can be testing times. These are interesting, testing times for clergy and for the people they serve.

Sour Grapes

Summer is high season for weddings, celebrity or otherwise. For the bride and groom, it's a day in a lifetime, usually. For a priest, it's an occupational hazard. Weddings are as popular as ever and the millennium year seems to be heading for vintage status. At least he won't forget the year, though all things are possible.

The whole idea of marriage has been deconstructed as social scientists might say. All of the patterns of our parents, or many of them at least have disappeared. Long years ago, marriages might have been loosely arranged, as they still are in many cultures. Families took a close interest in the match and families rather than individuals were joined in marriage. We look down our developed and progressive noses at the practice now but what alternative have we to offer from our times and our culture? Marriage chaos? Serial monogamy?

One of the differences which have arisen is the long-term planning which goes into a contemporary wedding. Most couples now buy their own property, furnish it, live together, sometimes have a child, and later get married. Living together was put forward in the recent past as a prevention of future break-up but the evidence for this is patchy at least.

The reality, though, is that most if not all couples effectively or actually live together before marriage now.

The seven-year itch syndrome, along with many other marriage dynamics seems to sunder many couples, whether they lived together or not before marriage. The emphasis on the material and on self-development, and self-fulfilment and the reduction in the number of children in contemporary relationships all affect the dynamic of modern marriage.

In a way, many of those who are getting married are more responsible than comparative couples in the past. Hard lessons have been learned in the past few decades. The potential for spouses and children to end up emotionally shredded is simply too great. Those living in violent, abusive unions are no longer expected to hide or to run for cover.

Couples are generally more realistic and therefore more cautious about commitment. Styles have become more subdued and less flamboyant too. Huge wedding bashes are generally out. Dress styles for the bride have become less voluminous and more streamlined and elegant. Arriving late is out as well. Even the ubiquitous video-camera is getting a rest sometimes in favour of still photographs.

Ceremonies are more carefully planned and acting on impulse is almost impossible because of new civil regulations.

One of the questions always asked of the priest is whether he gets fed up of all the wedding receptions. I don't know anyone in the vocation who expressly looks forward to them but most regard them as an opportunity to celebrate with parishioners and to honour families. The thought of another reception might not fill me with anticipation but they are part of what I do and I simply get on with it, hoping that they haven't put Auntie Florrie, who can talk to priests, beside me.

The ritual can get tiresome. Cards that have been sent by people who are present at the reception add to the never-ending pile which the groom's attendants read out. The waiting around for the photographer to take the positively last photograph, if so and so can be found. The average wait now between the start of the ceremony and the start of the meal is almost four hours. The turkey and ham is always predictable and seldom remarkable.

You could be forgiven for accusing me of sour grapes. Having never had the opportunity and running out of expectation, I am perhaps casting a cold eye on the whole experience. The truth is that for many people marriage is still entered into in good faith and with lofty idealism. Expectations within the relationship are similarly high and material pressures are many. Despite all this, it is usually a day which brings out the very best in everyone. People are generally in right relationship, at least for the moment, and it all leaves a warm glow of satisfaction in its aftermath.

Rubber turkey

One of my occupational hazards is getting stuck with the dinner guest 'from hell' to use a current television catch-phrase. If it happens to be a wedding guest then I am likely to be completely trapped as I am certain to be seated at the end of the table with literally no one to turn to. Formality still rules on special occasions and especially at weddings and I am most likely to end up beside a relative of the happy couple. Other guests choose their company, or are seated diplomatically according to table plan, but I pay for my honoured position by forfeiting my choice of company.

It may be one of the few occasions when an individual has to spend two hours or so talking with or listening to a priest, so I have some sympathy with them. There are at least some priests and religious with whom I wouldn't care to spend two hours. Being seated next to a priest may be a source of embarrassment for some, and for most, it is not something they would choose willingly and would avoid if they could only design the seating plan.

Whether it is a wedding or some other formal dinner function, the ritual has to be gone through. The priest says grace and the small talk begins. A safe topic is usually chosen first, to test the water, as it were. Where are you from? Where were you before? Do you like it here? On answering, 'Crossmaglen' to the first, I usually get a range of predictable responses, not usually including the latest one which took me completely by surprise, 'Crossmaglen, that's a lovely place'. Either she is an accomplished liar or a polished and automatic dispenser of the most banal of clichés. Having covered my curriculum vitae and assured my interrogator that previous postings were as nothing compared to my present one, the conversation can move on to more predictable and usual topics.

The scarcity of priests is an obvious one, since I have probably announced another later engagement as an escape strategy. Women priests, Bishop Casey and married clergy are the other high scorers. The dilemma is whether to agree with everything they say, in an effort to disarm them or to gently confront their arguments and prejudices and risk getting deeper into the mire. Some try to give you what they think you want to hear, and unleash a torrent of indignation at the 'state of religion in the country', the sins of 'young people nowadays', or any current public prejudice. I may get a sentimental history of their school days, of their altar-serving career, or of the priest who used to call to their house every week. They may not be religious themselves, (God forbid!), they assure you, but, 'once a catholic', and all that, world without end, Amen.

The greatest possible social mistake or faux-pas is to 'curse' in the company of the priest. My interrogator may be involved in all kinds of shady, sinful, immoral or illegal behaviours and there's no problem, but to swear in the company of the priest is the sin that cannot be forgiven, according to themselves. The public perception of the priest is revealed in the questions and assumptions. I am assumed to be from a middle or upper class upbringing, to have relatives who are priests, never to have worked in any other job, and to have been both celibate and single since birth. The priest is commonly assumed to be naïve, from an extremely sheltered background, and to be innocent of the 'real world'. He is thought to be easily impressed by shallow piousity, to be gullible, á la Father Dougal, and to be an innocent abroad, easily conned by sob stories and generally not to be taken too seriously. It is assumed that your life is rigidly governed by an autocratic parish priest and that your daily and nightly routine is fenced around by a multitude of inscrutable regulations and rules mostly concerned with what you cannot do.

Equally irritating is the guest who tries to impress you and others by ostentatiously dropping the 'Father' bit, calling you by your first name and swearing in your presence, just to prove that he, (it's usually a he), can, a little like a small child testing the boundaries. These are usually the same who make hackneyed jokes about confession or inflict their latest enthusiasm for some particular therapy or movement on you. Speaking of therapy, writing all the above, talking to an accepting, non judgemental blank and absorbing page has done me a world of good and left me ready to face the rubber chicken circuit again.

Brides behaving badly

Some time ago I was pacing impatiently up and down in the cemetery outside one of our churches waiting for the bride to arrive. It was forty-five minutes past the appointed hour and my blood-pressure was rising. The guests were mostly from other parts of the country. They too had arrived early and were seated patiently in the church. Most of us had been waiting for over an hour before the bride arrived. In an effort to lighten my mood I called one of the female altar servers whom I knew well and I asked her teasingly why it was that brides were invariably late for their weddings. She was well able to field my question and to return my teasing. She swivelled on her heels, struck a very feminine pose, complete with limp wrists and replied, 'beauty takes time!'

The problem of a bride arriving late for her wedding is not a new one. Late-coming is not always a problem but every so often serious delay occurs and takes the priest by surprise. It is sometimes the very person who protests that she is 'always early' who turns up late on the day. It is always someone else's fault of course. It was the traffic (everyone else got there on time); or the beautician (make-up can cover a multitude); the photographer (one last shot); the wedding car that arrived late or broke down (wasn't there any other car available?) or someone who forgot to bring the bouquets. I wonder what happens when a bride is late for the Registry Office appointment or for the honeymoon flight. The groom and his attendants are invariably early and available for snapshots and worn-out banter outside the church. Few ask how the prospective husband feels following the long wait for the Queen of Sheba to arrive. It is her big day. It is intended to be about two people and more but often only one claims the limelight. There is also the pastoral problem of families arriving late for baptisms and of the uncontrolled behaviour of children during the ceremonies.

In a marriage ceremony that is supposed to be centred on making promises, the first promise of the day (the promise to be on time, made several times at the wedding rehearsal) is invariably broken. Weary clergymen point out that the promise to sit down to the wedding reception in the hotel at a set time that evening is the next promise to hit the casualty list. On Saturday evenings I sometimes travel a distance to a wedding reception that begins late or moves slowly. I end up saying grace before meals, having soup and a bread-roll and setting off again on the journey home for evening Mass. The extraordinary thing is that people place such significance on the presence of clergy at the reception. If I have to explain that I cannot attend they often protest, 'but who will say grace?'

Another extraordinary feature of the wedding experience is the emphasis on formality. Every family wants to present the best possible face to the world on the day. In an informal world where social rules are minimal, the occasion of a wedding is highly structured and formalised. There is a specific place for everyone in a host of conventions and rules that simply cannot be broken. The bride's mother can hold the whole feminine attendance at the wedding to ransom by deciding to continue to wear or to remove her hat. Men folk at the top table often spend the whole mealtime worrying away their appetites. Their legs tremble under the table while they look visibly terrified at the prospect of having to make a speech in front of the worst possible audience - their family and friends.

Those who don't worry about their speech usually proceed to harass the guests by regaling them with every drunken escapade the speaker and 'the boys' had when they were at 'Uni'. They are also likely to use foul language, tell risqué jokes and recount episodes that might have been funny at the time but that have lost their humour in the interim. Families generally sit politely through the debacle of the speeches and the mind-numbing reading of the cards, but they are generally far from impressed by lewdness in speech on the occasion. The person most likely to ruin a wedding day is your Best Man.

One recent development is the use of the Internet for help in making speeches. I heard some Scots recently making wedding speeches that were peppered with Internet jokes. They attributed each joke, as they told them, to the web sites where they had found them. The joke I remember best was, 'What's the difference between an Irish wedding and an Irish wake?' The cheeky answer (from the Scots of all people) was that, 'there is one less drunk at the wake'.

Most couples plan their weddings very well and participate in them to a degree unknown to their parents, who generally had only to turn up at the church at the appointed time, often very early in the morning. Despite contemporary planning and careful rehearsals, things occasionally go wrong. The groom has a line in the ritual that begins, 'Wear this ring as a sign of my love and fidelity…' One hapless husband rendered this as, 'Wear this ring as a sign of my love and fertility…'! The same guy had no need to give any symbolic signs of his fertility.

The central parts of the marriage ceremony remain but details occasionally change. The throwing of confetti is no longer a problem for the sacristan. Black cats and horseshoes as symbols of good luck have gone out of fashion. They have been replaced by miniature bottles of bubbles, wedding candles, video recordings of the occasion and bagpipes at the reception. For the priest, it is just another day's work yet it is heartening for him to witness and share somehow in the general enthusiasm. The man playing the bagpipes often gets more in his brown envelope than the priest does and (presumably) he does not have to hand it in to the common fund when he gets home. When the couple have been cohabiting, as the vast majority do nowadays, it is sometimes hard to see where they get the enthusiasm to organise and celebrate the occasion of their wedding. Someone recently pointed out to me that paradoxically, it is a sign of real love when a couple get married having already spent several years together. 'Man', they say, 'is incomplete until he enters into the complementary relationship with a woman that is marriage'. 'Then', it is said, – 'he is finished!'

The silent treatment

Going on retreat is part of the rhythm of most priests' lives. The term retreat is perhaps coloured by its military associations. My retreat is not, in the military sense, a withdrawal from the struggle, or a shying away from the fight. It is more like that which is termed a 'tactical retreat', a temporary withdrawal to a place of quiet so as to regroup and to replenish resources. It is an opportunity for intensive preparation to renew myself for the daily challenge which is life.

With this idealism in mind, I headed for Burnfoot, Co Donegal, to my 'locus refugii', my place of refuge, as penal bishops used to describe their present address. The retreat centre provides monk-like cells in which those of solitary disposition can spend some quiet time. A resident female hermit provides inspiration by silent example when the solitary life begins to lose its appeal.

I arrived, after a particularly intense few months of pastoral work, to a certain confusion regarding my identity. 'No', I explained to the director, 'I'm not from R.T.E.'. In the later quiet, it came to mind that this has happened to me before. I will have to change my accent or my pronunciation in future, or learn to articulate properly the name of the parish in which I live and work, as the locals do. Ath-ir-dee, not R.T.E.

I was assigned Mark II, the cells being named after the four evangelists. All my wandering mind could think of is which of the Ford Cortinas of my teen years was the Mark II. For some years past, I had been assigned to Luke one and two, and the unfamiliarity of Mark initially grated. Like a cow deprived of its usual stall, I had to get familiarised with the geography of new surroundings, even if it was only a single cell room. The dramatic scenery of the Donegal landscape provided the backdrop against which the inner drama of my soul was to take place. The music was that of the dawn chorus, and the sound effects were provided by Easter lambs.

I missed having to attend to the voracious appetite of the barrel-stove in the corner. This time round, May sunshine provided the heat. The turf-scented smoke of the stove had incensed my previous year's thoughts. Its licking, leaping flames had provided ever-changing colour and form to the darkness of my night-time existence and sparks to ignite my imagination. It had also secured me from the external drama of winter weather.

Deprived of the usual stimuli of radio and television, inner thoughts and conversations run riot. Night-time and the struggle begins to bring order meaning and control to the waves of ideas, memories and fantasies which wash over the quieted mind. It is relatively easy, they say, to do good deeds, but difficult to think good thoughts.

As the muddied waters of the daytime mind settle, and the worldly sediment falls to the bottom and congeals, the floating debris of the conscious mind can be fished out and examined. No longer weighted down or anchored by the ballast of everyday routine, the unconscious has given up some of its encrusted treasure, to be examined in the bright light of conscious judgement. Emotional clarity and understanding soaks through the stillness. Action is promised out of the still silence. Some insight and a temporary victory over the demons may be achieved in my solitary desert struggle.

The silent treatment is not for the easily bored. Silence is something we occasionally inflict on each other in anger as passive aggression and punishment. Occasionally, in reaction to stress, we may be stunned into silence or we take temporary silence on ourselves as a refuge from a noise-filled world and as reward and then only in small doses. I observe my hermit neighbour and wonder how a lifetime of solitude and silence can be achieved. Are my four days retreat to be thought of as penance or privilege, as a freedom or a duty? The Greek philosopher Socrates gave us an answer many, many centuries ago. He said, 'The unexamined life is not worth living'.

Michael Murtagh

Black priests and white babies

The late Cardinal Tómas Ó Fiaich once famously suggested that, because of falling numbers of vocations, the day would come when black priests would come to minister among us. I'm sure he meant this as a throw-away remark. It was not a prophecy or a thought out policy. It evoked sensation however and the Cardinal stood accused of racism. The word 'black' was not politically correct at the time. Some questioned why the prospect of black priests or indeed priests of any other shade working among us should be used in such an alarmist way. Surely there was a subtle racism in the sensationalism. If the African people could accept, even welcome Irish priests and clergy, why might we not reciprocate their generosity? Perhaps it was a question of Irish pride, pride of a churchy kind especially.

For several years now, I have had to brief African priests who have come to work temporarily here in Co. Louth. They come to study and work at weekends and in holiday times. People often remember the Cardinal's remarks and repeat them and I wished these priests to know what was being referred to. The present priest, Fr Jude, an African Igbo, intends to be here for the two year duration of his studies. 'Reverse Mission' is the term the verbal technicians give to this phenomenon. Quietly, almost surreptitiously, the black priest has arrived.

Though interesting, the arrival of the black priest is by no means an answer to the vocations deficit. The 'ship them in' answer to personnel deficits is not an adequate response. European missionaries eventually recognised that the health and the future of the church in Africa and elsewhere depended on indigenous or local clergy. The foreign graft seldom 'takes' as successfully as the local. Having expressed the reservation, and dampened the sensationalism, the experience of working with an African 'brother' is enriching, mutually so I hope. Seeing ourselves through the eyes of others is a fascinating if not always flattering exercise. As we are fascinated by the personalities of others, so the religious and social personality of our people, as reflected back to us can be revealing.

Having discussed our silent and reticent manner in church, and having analysed the 'back of the chapel' attitude many times, I still cannot adequately explain our restrained and self-conscious behaviour. We blame our shyness on post colonial syndrome, and our behaviour in chapel as a relic of penal times or of class ridden yesterdays when we knew our place and it was at the back. Stepping out of line by being conspicuous or putting our head over the social parapet by getting involved left a person open to social comment of the caustic or begrudging kind. There is no easy explanation of what others see as the split between our exuberance at sport or at music and the 'cold-ness' and oppressive atmosphere of our liturgical behaviour.

The foreign eye often sees strengths in our care of the sick and the old. We are universally regarded as generous and faith-filled. It also sees the glaring deficiencies; the culture of alcohol; the rising individualism or self-ism; the crumbling of community and family, and the extravagant waste. The weather, our national obsession, does not encourage immigrants. These African priests come to learn. They end up teaching those who have ears to listen. We have much to teach them and more to learn from them. We are an old and sometimes wise church, they a new one. Like the old we can also sometimes or oftener become paralysed by over cautiousness, or become complacent and opinionated. Meanwhile Ardee meets Africa, Africa meets Ardee.

Talking nonsense

'Silence is indeed the helper and friend of thought and invention but if one aims at readiness of speech and beauty of discourse he will get at them by no other discipline than the study of words and their constant practice'.

This quote from an ancient author came to mind as I knuckled down to the task of choosing words once again for the many and varied occasions during an average week when I am called on to articulate the grief or happiness of a family or community. There are the regular occasions like the Sunday homily with time to prepare and research the texts beforehand. There are the more pressing occasions like funerals when the text has to be prepared with less time and there are a myriad of other occasions when words are called for. The composition, preparation and delivery of words can be daunting, especially for those unused to the process. I have sat beside too many nervous wedding guests dreading the 'few words' expected of them to forget this. The use of words can also be amusing and witty and the words we use and the way we use them tells us a lot about national character. The number of new words that enter the public vocabulary in the wake of technology is constantly growing. Some of them, unintentionally perhaps, are self contradictory and therefore funny. The technical term for these verbal self contradictions are 'oxymorons'.

A sample, my worst favourite, to begin with, is the lady who described her unmarried daughter as slightly pregnant. Maybe she was absolutely unsure or it may have been an accurate estimate of her daughter's maternal condition. She discovered later that she was almost exactly right. It was a shame, she thought, as her daughter was awful nice and had been among the first in her class at school. It was undoubtedly all the fault of that adult male her daughter had been dating recently. She had told her friends about this mature student, a sensitive man who was apparently also a rap artist, whom she had met at college. It could not have been a deliberate mistake on her part as he had claimed. She is clearly confused.

The world of politics and that of journalism which often feeds off it are awash with such oxymorons and nonsense talk. The truth is that we are often taken in by the word spinning of those whose craft is to sculpture words and phrases that keep the entire truth from us. Religion has its fair share too, as in that phrase so beloved of Ulster Unionists, Roman Catholic

– with the emphasis heavy on the Rome. Is it possible to be catholic and Roman? Are the terms Democratic Unionist or I.R.A. peace initiative more of the genre? We may have to agree to disagree. Same difference. Can one be gospel greedy or devilishly good and is it possible to accurately describe someone as a Jesus freak? Is there such a thing as a short sermon or a lovely service? Miley of Glenroe was famous for his 'Holy God' spake but the four letter words that commonly follow holy.... in everyday exclamations usually has little to do with things holy. It's a holy terror what people do to language, even religious language. And as for that other oxymoron, Reverend (supply your own example!)

It would be a brave politician who would go against the advice of his civil servants. I mean the ones who write to us 'Dear Client, threat, threat, threat, etc and finish off with, 'your obedient servant' etc. There would undoubtedly be civil war if such should happen. Politicians use oxymorons so regularly that they no longer notice the irony in their speech. Negative growth means that we are in a recession. Rising deficits are bad for the economy. Temporary tax increases are thought to be necessary. Peace keeping forces are routinely sent to trouble spots along with mild mannered reporters speaking of journalistic integrity. The rules of war, or is it low intensity conflict, are invoked, if seldom kept. Army intelligence has all the answers. The days of benevolent dictators are spoken of wistfully by those with short memories. It is all pleasantly confusing.

Some of these nonsense words are international, like Australian culture or American education or Great Britain. Others are local to the point of being understood only in certain provinces or parishes. Where I come from we describe a youth with an old head on his shoulders as an 'auld man gassan'. In the north of the country you can meet wild quiet people, people who are pure evil, fierce holy women and ordinary decent criminals. You can meet baldy-haired men, men with hair like steel wool, and you get death benefits when you die. You can drink dry wine and find easy-to-follow instructions on the carton.

A people of the Exodus

Today I had an uninterrupted hour of quiet meditation – in the confession box. Easter and the recent devotions to Divine Mercy appear to have mopped up all the potential penitents. There were no slides opening or shutting reluctantly over the grilles; no muffled shuffling and clearing of throats as people found their kneeling place when the internal light in the box extinguished; no whispered admissions of failure filling my ears full of sins. I had unlocked only one side of the box. I wasn't expecting a crowd. Confession boxes are locked nowadays for security. It seems that there are some who want to enter the box to commit sin rather than to confess sin. It's not quite that confession has become extinct. It is forming different patterns. There was a decent attendance, as usual, at the community celebrations of the sacrament around Easter time. The old patterns of Saturday midday confession, weekly or monthly, are all but gone. A new pattern has emerged of less frequent, more personal and generally more realistic confession has taken its place, where people have substituted anything at all in place of the old habits. It is the same with Mass-going. Numbers are not in free-fall though there are swathes missing, yet special events still draw big crowds who are often publicly appreciative of the liturgies prepared for them - at funerals and weddings for example.

The statistics industry continues to paint a bleak landscape for the present and for the foreseeable future in terms of numbers. The evidence is most obvious with regard to church personnel. There is a huge gap looming which means that serving priests will not be replaced easily and the age profile of present personnel is top-heavy. I doubt if priests will still be sitting in silent confession boxes on Saturdays in a few years time or saying Mass for half a dozen people in country churches on winter mornings. Change will undoubtedly come in its most painful form. It will force itself on a reluctant church community.

I often say that it's a good thing for the priest to go to Mass occasionally. I mean that he should attend as a regular member of the congregation. This can be a revealing and sometimes painful experience. The priest, like any professional, is usually more finely tuned to the mechanics of the liturgy and may spend his time mentally comparing styles and competence. It is hard to avoid the 'what I would have said or done' line of thought. Having achieved control over the internal critic you begin to experience the feelings of consolation and irritation that sitting in a pew involves.

There are the practical things like the draught that threatens to cut your head off at the neck or the stiff church furniture that refuses to bend or mould itself to your aching frame. This is an experience well-known to the priest in the presiding chair too. Who ever thought of making the presider's chair out of cold marble and with a short back so that your spine is in danger of being severed if you sit back? There are the doors that bang shut after the latecomers who then push those already in the pew over so as to make room, leaving you blinded by a pillar and trapped on the far inside in a side-aisle seat with sound but no picture. There is the calculation as to when it is best to leave the seat to receive communion and the conundrum as to how to recognize your seat on the way back. If you get trapped behind a child who is at the exploratory stage you can spend your entire time making funny faces or doing battle with uncharitable thoughts. If your somewhat deaf neighbour is at the other end of the developmental scale you may find yourself listening to the priest and to his time-delayed echo as your friend says mass with him.

The presiding priest may be one of those priests who are determined to stamp their personality on proceedings and begins with a forced cheeriness that can be so tiresome. 'Good Morning everyone' he inevitably begins. 'Good Morning Fath-er' the herd inevitably intones like a class of four year olds. The first ten seconds are make-or-break time. The presiding priest sets the tone for the next forty minutes or so. It will either be a prayerful, professional, reflective, unfolding of the Mass or the liturgy involved or it will be a sloppily presented, badly prepared, going-through-the-motions, dispiriting chore, slow to the point of dragging. Alternatively, it may be a crowd-pleasing 'fast Mass'. If the presider decides to jolly things up and to tackle boredom head-on, then prepare for the equivalent of a game-show host and a liturgy performance that puts his personality centre-stage as he regularly interrupts with his own spin on what is going on.

Of course the congregation affects the quality of the liturgy too. All the preparation and prayerfulness in the world on the part of the priest will fall flat in the face of a reluctant, passive, statue-like congregation who will neither act nor react to any stimulus. There are congregations that treat you like a leper and will not approach where you stand. There are the latecomers who arrive with the same precise degree of lateness every day. There are the clock-watchers; the terminally bored; the over-enthusiastic responders; the holders-up of internal or external walls; the people of the Exodus leaving at Holy Communion time as if a fire had broken out; the conversational types or the rosary-sayers who blithely ignore your carefully prepared words and whistle and whisper their way through the homily.

The opportunity of a weekly audience with at least part of the community is something many groups would prize highly and use efficiently. The difficulty for priests and for people in the pews is that we are trying to communicate to a people who have largely been reared in an audio-visual age. The degree of professionalism and the extent of stimulation that a contemporary audience is exposed to mean that First Mass on Sunday morning can never match up to the entertainment of Saturday night. The threshold of boredom is so lowered that if the congregation were to be supplied with remote controls, priests would be zapped off screen regularly. We cannot hope to compete with the wall-to-wall entertainment that is contemporary culture. Our space and pace is different and we shouldn't fall into the trap of taking on the worst of the showbusiness industry. We can, of course, take on its skills and professionalism and use them to our benefit and to that of the congregation. Contemporary congregations are used to professional standards of communication and connectedness. They are no longer the submissive, uncritical, 'pray, pay and obey' crowds of the past. They have matured in the suffering and in the storms of recent times and they will affirm or confront you more often. Their expectations are high. Their demands are challenging. Their allegiance cannot be taken for granted. They come to the well expecting not to go away thirsty.

In the interests of religion....

'Any word of the changes'? is a question associated with this time of the year within the world of diocesan clergy. The ordinations, if any, are generally over and the holidays have not quite begun. When the changes are 'out', the speculation regarding placements dies and the holiday season really begins. The anxiety obviously generated by the prospect of a change or by the absence of change is part of the life and conversation of diocesan priesthood. The question of change is one parishioners frequently ask about too. Can you be changed from here at any time, they ask, obviously intrigued by the impermanence of our existence.

Our fellow priests who are organised in religious orders rather than by diocese have different systems. Their structure allows for what they call 'chapter' every five years or thereabouts. This is essentially a convention where leaders are elected and positions within the organisation are filled for a specific number of years. If they prove good at their job they may be re-elected to office for another term at the next chapter before returning to the ranks. The internal politics of these elections gives rise to the same speculation and uncertainty as in diocesan life. The difference is that each member of the order has some kind of say in the leadership of their group and the decision that is eventually made can be unmade at the next chapter.

The general question of change in the life of a priest intrigues people whose lives are lived in a stable, unchanging pattern and in an environment which remains essentially the same over the course of their lifetime. Having to change the area in which you work, the people with whom you associate, and the general pattern of your life can be a daunting prospect, especially for those who do not live with that expectation. Most priests live with the knowledge that their present circumstances are temporary and when change comes it does not cause the anxiety or psychological displacement that it might for others. A change in vocational or work circumstances can be traumatic yet most priests cope well with the reality of their impermanence. Their roots are not sunk in their adoptive community in the same way as those of their parishioners or the residents of that area. The priest will have lived in several different communities over a lifetime and there are usually no family or property ties to the parish in which they work.

'Do you have any say'? people ask, or 'Can you be changed at any time'? The answer to the first question is that times are changing and the days of getting a letter in the post telling you to be in Dundalk or somewhere else within the Archdiocese are gone. The Archbishop has the final say and junior clergy mostly do not argue but there is generally more consultation and dialogue now and changes do not arrive in the morning post the day before the Bishop goes on holiday. In other days the notice of change came in a standard letter that began, 'In the interests of religion…'

There is a contemporary problem, in that because of the ever diminishing pool of diocesan clergy, the bishop does not have the same sanctions open to him as in the past and clergy are beginning to attempt to pick and choose where they will serve, a development which seems to me to be contrary to their vocation. There is a double-edged responsibility here. There is an onus on clergy to be available in accord with the needs of the gospel in any particular situation and an obligation on bishops to be pastorally knowledgeable and sensitive to the human gifts and to the failings of those priests in their charge.

The answer to part two of the query is that curates can be changed at any time. Parish Priests have some security in their post but they also may be asked to change. The change to parish priest is generally made in line with seniority, the 'chief waiters' being those longest ordained and not yet appointed to their own parish. The average age at which a priest is given a parish has fallen a little in recent decades and a priest can now expect to be made parish priest in his late forties or early fifties. The log-jam and the human waste that arises from this model of people management has long been debated but never been effectively tackled.

The greatest anxiety that emerges from the changes is the lack of pattern in the transfers that are made. American diocesans speak of the, 'billiard ball approach' where there is a general scattering with a hope that some good will come from the random nature of the spray. The 'bush in the gap' approach which places people in vacant positions regardless of suitability in talent or temperament is more common nowadays than the scattering which was possible when personnel were more numerous and more pliant. The management of what industry calls human resources calls for delicacy of approach and depth of knowledge of human nature and neither of the above models allows for these. Making personnel changes for the sake of change or for less worthy motives such as the exercise of power, punitive changes or moving problems elsewhere (the geographical approach) have all been experienced at some time. The more cautious minimalist approach to change, that is, a policy of as little change as possible, is equally stifling and it becomes a recipe for stagnation and inertia.

Whatever the Summer brings in the way of change or in the dynamics of changing personnel we have to be more optimistic than the French in their famous proverb, 'Plus ça change, plus c'est la même chose'- the more things change the more they stay the same.

Father's Day

The parent of an adult family said to me recently that while her own parents and their generation was commonly thought to have had life hard, she believed that her, now middle-aged generation, have an even harder time. She explained that the deprivation her parents had endured was largely material while the confusion, the suffering and the deprivation of her contemporaries was largely emotional. Material improvements, progress and development over time has eradicated most of the poverty and the hard grind of daily life and labour which had been the lot of most of our parents or grandparents. The scarcity of opportunity and prospects for most people has largely been removed by access to high-quality education. While the disadvantages of our grandparents' time were considerable, the hardships that marked her generation, she said, were more difficult to overcome, because they belong largely to the realm of the complex, intangible world of feelings.

She explained her insight in terms of the rejection and confusion that contemporary parents feel when their adult children reject the values and the standards of behaviour that had been taught to them. In the name of freedom of expression or of bogus rights to happiness, a generation has cast aside the cultural habits and the moral underpinning which had been so important to generations of fore-parents. The fracture between the generations has proved painful. These parents no longer expect the comfort of cultural continuity. The feelings of guilt, of confusion, of failure and of rejection which this has left them with, were, she said, a greater burden than the material deprivation that marked the lives of a previous generation.

I find that this is true in that parents of her generation often ask priests what they can or should do when their children reject the ways and habits of faith, when they behave in ways that their parents, and most of the rest of the world, consider scandalous and when they fail to take seriously or completely disregard the heartbreak of their parents. Parents often express the deep pain they feel when the values that form the core of their very identities are rejected. The experience of these deserted parents often comes close to desolation. Their very identity is so aligned to their religious and cultural beliefs, that to reject one is to reject the other. I usually try to assure them that they have probably done all they could in terms of rearing their children and have done it well and they must let go of feelings of responsibility or guilt for their adult children's often self-indulgent behaviours.

I encourage them not to judge those who may have judged them as old-fashioned and out-of-touch, not to reject those who have, perhaps unwittingly, rejected the very identity and sense of self of their parents, and to simply try to explain to their adult children, at an appropriate time, the sadness, the rejection, the pain and the bewilderment they feel. I find that parents are often caught in the horns of a dilemma of how to take a stand for their own values while trying not to alienate their children, by voicing their disapproval of their behaviour. These parents often feel at an educational disadvantage. They feel they have not had the same benefits and privileges of education and travel that their children have enjoyed and are at a loss to reply adequately to their progeny's dismissive and sometimes cynical arguments and questions. They feel that the wisdom they have to offer is dismissed and they intuitively feel that the world-view and lifestyle that has replaced their vision of life is superficial and hollow. They often end up picking up the emotional bill by looking after displaced grandchildren or deserted and separated sons and daughters.

Not only do such parents feel personally dismissed or rejected, they feel that the life and times of their whole post-war generation has been vilified. There has been a soap-powder 'ad' approach to their history. The analysis is that in our parents' repressed society and times, everything was stained, soiled, and positively stinking. A dash of new improved modernity, a quick spin, and see the difference. Contemporary attitudes and lifestyles are held up to the light and they are demonstrated to be sparkling white, whiter than white, even a little smug and self-righteous. These middle-aged parents feel that a generation which prides itself on being emotionally literate and 'tuned in' is most often stranded and stuck, their antennae permanently locked on to the station marked 'self'.

Before the Father's Day cards buckle, wilt and fall off the family mantle-piece into the consuming fire, take time to discover what the generation who reared you feel and think. Ask them what they have experienced and what life has taught them. You may have the experience that the writer Mark Twain spoke of when he told the story of how, when he was a teenager, having had a row with his father, he decided his father knew nothing about anything and was generally, 'for the birds'. Some years later, as a young adult he went for a long walk and thought hard about his father again. After much deliberation he decided that, in the years that had passed since his earlier thoughts and verdict, his father had learnt a great deal.

What might have been

It is Easter Sunday morning. The marathon church services of the Easter vigil are over. My early morning rota of Masses is said and the prospect of a quiet, restful week looms. There is a lift in my heart. My spirits are buoyed by the church liturgy and by my own rhetoric about the Easter triumph over suffering and death. Good Friday has been overcome and Holy Saturday has been seen through. The brightness of the morning and the resurrection of the bursting buds and leaves and flowers from their winter death allow hope and joy to rise within me, giving me life, like the rising sap of springtime. I exchange Easter greetings with familiar faces and head home for coffee, to lift my energy levels as well as my spirits.

The coffee break is interrupted by a message that a phone call from the emergency services arrived while I was out. I call back and receive the predictable call-out. Having liaised with the Gardai, we plan to break the tragic news of a fatality together to the family. I have suddenly become part of a drama which is every parent's nightmare, the knock on the door which tells them their adult child has been killed in a road traffic accident, an R.T.A. in professional speak. We drive the short distance to the family home and drop our verbal bombshell. There is no easy way of dropping a bombshell and the results are always devasting. The routine of a Sunday morning is abandoned. We are all suddenly back to Good Friday.

I watch parents overcome with shock and grief trying to piece together the movements and the company of their child who did not return from the party. Waves of grief, pangs of guilt and self-reproach and hints of anger flash across their tearfilled expressions. Their questions are answered quietly, professionally and honestly by the professionals present. After the initial shock and the gradual realisation of all that has happened, there are procedures to be gone through, relatives to be summoned, and practicalities to be looked after.

Like most parents they have done everything they could to protect their family. They have worried about their safety and been told that they were over-protective, over-reacting. They have watched and waited and called the homes of friends trying to trace them when they did not return at night. They have learned that youth has the power and the finance to live independently of them and they have chosen to allow them to remain living at home as far as possible. They have no wish to drive their children to resentment. Like many parents they often feel powerless in the face of the dangers, challenges and opportunities open to their children. There are few sanctions available to the parents, few controls which can be realistically enforced.

The immediate agony of the breaking news gives way over the course of the day to the bleakness of the Holy Saturday experience. The four saddest words in the English language, 'what might have been' are explored wistfully. A sense of hollowness fills the atmosphere. The story is told and retold so that the reality of death and the finality of the separation might eventually sink in. Small knots of men and of women huddle together for mutual support and fall into traditional roles of carers and providers.

The weekend blend of youth, fearlessness, partying and vehicles has once again proven to be a lethal cocktail. The fears of parents have proven to be well-founded. The celebration of the present moment without care for the future, so distinctive of youth, has turned into tragedy. Our roads have once again proved to be the end of the road for an individual's dream and for the dreams of a family. The insistent growth of the death tally seems to be of little or no deterrent value. Every bad bend, every accident blackspot, every scene of fatality leaves a legacy of lifetime brokenness. Wayside shrines with their crosses and flowers turn our roads into a Via Dolorosa, a stations of the cross.

It is less easy to speak of Easter joy now. The spirit of joy and hope give way to sombre and sobering thoughts. Holy Week has arrived again and it has to be lived through again. It seems that there is no other way except that which leads through suffering. We are indeed slow to learn.

Death on the radar

There is a saying that the old go to their death but death comes to the young. The week that has just passed has been overshadowed for me by the cruel and poignant death of two young people, one a parishioner, in a road traffic accident. Their story was overlain with added poignancy in that they were about to leave for Dublin airport to begin a year-long trip to Thailand and Australia. The accident that ended their lives and shattered their dreams happened at Monasterboice. Their car, intending to turn right into the girl's home, was hit from behind and thrown into the path of an oncoming lorry. Both families were waiting nearby. They witnessed the fire, the flames and the smoke that resulted. Much of what had been their lives went up with those flames and that smoke. I officiated at a joint funeral Mass for both victims and at a prayer service for the bereaved the night before the funeral Mass. There were, as expected, many young people present. Some people had also held a prayer vigil at the scene of the accident and both homes were inundated with visitors paying their respects.

At times like these there is a natural and touching concern for parents. Adult children often ask me to pray for their parents that they may get through the trauma of a tragic death, the funeral and the bereavement that follows. I try to reassure them, where it is appropriate, that their parents, however traumatised, have strengths and resources that younger people simply do not have access to. 'It will kill my parents', people say. We forget that our parents have lived longer, seen and experienced more and can usually call on deposits of faith and reserves of spiritual capital. Death is generally no stranger to them even if it is a most unwelcome intruder. We can be naïve, idealistic, even patronising regarding our parents, their strengths, their weaknesses and their personal histories.

The younger people I saw at the various liturgies were perhaps in a greater state of confusion than most of the parents present. Death was generally not on the radar of their lives at all. This may have been the closest contact they have ever had with the brutal reality of sudden or accidental death. They simply did not have the same coping skills as their parents, the emotional shock absorbers that develop with experience, with lived life. They had been used to planning and achieving, to ordering their lives and their futures without the interruption of tragedy or the radical uncertainty that marks life for most people.

The church was full and overflowing for all the liturgies that were held during the week. Many of those present were peers of the young couple. The language of the church came into strangely sharp focus despite the emotional gloom of the occasion. In the November mist, the autumnal chill, the religious images used seemed sharper and clearer. This unspeakable death is what we wish to be redeemed from. This unimaginable ending to an adventure, to a story of love is what we want to be saved from. With the backdrop of tragedy the religious set and furnishings, the fixtures and fittings of ritual communicated.

The church has a power to dignify death somehow. The funeral ritual still speaks to people. They may not all listen attentively or retain and internalise the message. They may forget or distort or disregard the meaning. They may return to old habits of laziness and apathy. Much of the seed sown may be lost but much of the abundant seed of nature is lost too. Enough of the seeds of hope and faith always fall on fertile ground to allow life and faith to continue.

The initial denials of the reality of what had happened were followed by the numbness that intelligent nature provides to anaesthetise us temporarily from the pain and from the full impact of tragedy. Grief has its own dynamic, its own ways and laws and I began to observe the process in its earliest stages.

Patrick Kavanagh wrote that we do not, 'architecture our grief'. There may be common patterns but grief flows spontaneously and follows no set plan for the individual. Each bereavement is unique and is lived through the prism of each irreplaceable personality. It is experienced in a special, personal way because each person's experience is a new and unrepeated pattern. Some of the anger that can follow bereavement flashed through momentarily. Anger can be misdirected on to doctors or priests and most professionals learn to absorb, to be as a sponge, soaking up the emotional discharge. Questioning follows too. The 'whys' of tragedy are generally without answer. The early days are not times for philosophising or for deep reasoning. I let the questions go to the goalie. Those who are grieving sometimes try to strike bargains with God in bereavement. Promises can be rashly made. 'I'll visit the grave every day' can turn into an occasion of guilt when this becomes impractical. Guilt, another of the fruits of bereavement emerges in the tortured thoughts of, 'what might have been'. These words are said to be the four saddest words in the

English language. Acceptance comes slowly. The running wound heals over. An ugly scar remains, an emotional disfigurement, with nerve ends that are over-sensitive to the slightest cue. The most ordinary of associations can cause the grieving mind to flood once again with a torrent of painful memories.

The images of a week of tragedy and bereavement are not easily erased. I saw the familiar faces of mothers become almost unrecognisable, disfigured and contorted by the pain of losing an adult child, suffering in their going. I saw young faces frozen, staring blankly and piercingly, emotionally shredded, seized by the onslaught on their senses and on their emotions. I saw fathers and brothers shouldering the burden as men do in their own fashion, getting practicalities sorted, reserving emotional expression for more private moments. I saw neighbours, women mostly, managing the regression of a grieving household, allowing their kin and friends to labour in despair that they might give birth to hope. Time heals it is said. Time can also hurt. An instant of carelessness, ill-judgement or bad luck can unleash a lifetime of regret, pain and loss. One instant can change everything.

Michael Murtagh

Bad things and good people

The death of the Tyrone captain, Cormac Mc Anallan, 'a good solid lad' in the words of his brother, has caught the attention of a shocked public. Cormac's high profile ensured that his sudden and inexplicable death received much publicity. This and the recent deaths of some other young people, especially young men, reminded me of a book that was written by a religious man, Rabbi Harold Kushner, following the death of his teenage son. He called the book, 'When bad things happen to good people'. He describes the question as to why bad things happen to good people as the only one question that really matters. He observed that every meaningful conversation with others about religion or about God eventually gets around to this question or begins with it. He writes that, 'Most thinking people are troubled by the unfair distribution of suffering in the world. The misfortunes of others are not just a problem to those who are suffering and to their families. They are a problem to everyone who wants to believe in a just and fair and liveable world. They inevitably raise questions about the goodness, the kindness, even the existence of God'.

It is said that only the neurotic expect the world to be fair yet we do expect a measure of justice in all that happens and young people especially are very finely tuned to the concept of justice. That is what makes them so indignant at the compromises and excuses that mark adult adaptation to the world and that makes them cry out, 'it's not fair' so frequently. Some people try to explain tragedy away by protesting that we get what we deserve, that misfortune is punishment. This keeps their world orderly and understandable and keeps both the carrot and the stick in place, encouraging us to do good and giving fearful motive to avoid wrongdoing. It is a neat and attractive solution but it does not fit the facts. It encourages people to blame themselves and perhaps to hate God. Others say that justice comes in the long run but it may be too late by then for most who suffer and many do not live to see justice restored. 'Grand Designs' have inflicted much misery on multitudes of individuals whether these plans come good or otherwise in the long term. In the meantime, the wrong people get sick, are hurt or die.

Some say that suffering is purposeful, educational or purifying. It may be to some degree but the argument that runs along these lines is primarily meant to defend God. It unintentionally portrays God as playing games with the lives of people and it does not really help the sufferer or explain the predicament.

Those who explain suffering as God's way of changing us are seldom clear as to what it is that God wants changed. Others use the 'broad back' explanation, saying that God has recognised some spiritual strength in people and sent them tragedy, that God never sends more of a burden than people can bear. Experience, sadly, teaches us otherwise. Some people crack under the strain of unbearable tragedy. Some people become more noble and sensitive. Others become jealous of the good fortune of others or they become cynical and bitter. Relationships sometimes break up under the strain and the blame. If God is testing people, many fail the test. If God is distributing burdens, there is more than the occasional miscalculation.

One of the things that disturb me is the trite and presumptuous explanation, in times of fatality, that tragedy has come to liberate us from a world of pain and to bring us to a better, more peaceful place. When all else fails, welcome heaven. There is one often-used communion reflection that begins, 'Death is nothing at all'. Try telling that with a straight face to the hurt and angry mourners in the front seat who have just lost a child in tragic circumstances. Faith in a world where all things are put right can be of great comfort to a suffering and bereaved family but it can also be an excuse for not grappling with the injustice of life and for not using our God-given intelligence and resources to develop and to wrestle with difficulties rather than for war-making for example.

Some things happen for no discernible reason. The world and nature are both orderly and sometimes chaotic. What we need to do is to try our best to prevent tragedies happening again, to use our human freedom well and for the good and to use our knowledge and wisdom to help those for whom it is too late and to improve preventative medicine or similar projects. We also need to recognise what may be our own contribution to tragedy and not to dump on God in all circumstances. God cannot be responsible for all of life's tragedies. There can be a certain random-ness about tragedy or death. The grim reaper can sweep all before him. There are no exceptions for nice people and there is no escape from mortality. We need to rise above the question, 'why did it happen' and begin to ask the question, 'what do I do now that it has happened?'

One of the phrases that have entered our general vocabulary from the Old Testament is that of 'Job's comforters'. These are the people who arrive at the house of trouble, armed with advice rather than sympathy. People need compassion in tragic circumstances more than they need explanations or advice or tales of similar, Olympic-scale stories of suffering from the life of the would-be comforter. We have all heard the stock phrases: Don't take it so hard; don't fly in the face of God; H/she has gone to a better place; it could be worse. These genuine attempts at comforting the bereaved can be misguided and unappreciated. The bereaved need listeners rather than talkers. They need permission to be angry rather than soothers who order them to be paragons of patience and piety. They need to be freed from guilt rather than to be loaded with more misgivings.

People going through a hard time need consolation more than explanation. They need the reassurance that they are good people and do not deserve what has happened to them. They need to find meaning in suffering and to put it in context. Community gets people through trauma. God sends people to sit with us through grief. Religion puts us in touch with others as much as it puts us in touch with God. With tragedy we do not need so much to explain it, to justify it or to accept it but to survive it, to recognise its unfairness and to go on living. The really important question is not why bad things happen but where will we find the resources to cope when they do happen.

God does not always send the problems. Some are caused by bad luck or bad people or imperfect nature but God may provide the strength and the personal resources to deal with problems. God may be as outraged as we are by tragedy and suffering. We need to forgive nature for not being perfect; to stop blaming God for not organising a better world; to reach out to those afflicted around us and to go on living despite it all.

Number two, please

Feeling the need to alter my image, I took myself off recently for one of my increasingly rarer visits to the barber for a haircut. I can only bow to the power of nature and order a short haircut nowadays, or in the language of contemporary barbers and their younger customers, a number two or a number four. The number apparently refers to the gauge of the blades used.

I'm inclined to carry out all my non-priestly business dressed in civilian or casual clothes. I like the anonymity and the freedom of being unidentifiable or typecast. The barber shop I chose seemed like a regular male barber shop the last time I visited. It was sparse and basic, a shade inaccessible and with a rapid turnover of males whose hirsute needs could be taken care of in a matter of minutes.

I entered and sat for a while, reading the newspaper and hoping that most of it wouldn't stay on my hands. A young boy, meanwhile, was throwing the mother of all tantrums, as a male barber and the child's mother tried to distract him while trying to cut his hair without cutting his head. At the other end of the shop a female barber was finishing off her latest assignment and seeing her customer off.

She invited me to take a seat at her end of the salon and as she promptly returned she asked me, and gently suggested to me at the same time, that what I needed was a general tidying up. Precisely.

She made it known to me immediately that she was a talking barber. This was no sullen male, occasionally venturing into the safe male domains of football, cars or holidays but a woman with views and with a view to expressing them. She began on current affairs, the Russian submarine story. She immediately tried to establish some kind of rapport by using very strong language, saying that her sympathy lay not with the political or military establishment in Russia but with those trapped, the poor so and so's in the submarine. I felt a little trapped myself, being wrapped mummy-like by now, and feeling a little out of my depth. I nodded compliantly and murmured approvingly as the conversation quickly surfed several topics.

This was a travelled woman and she aired her views on 'Jew-boys', on 'Paki's', 'who resented every penny they spent on a haircut', on Turks, 'the best barbers in the world, using a razor', and on male barbers generally, whom, she opined, 'couldn't cut long hair properly'. It hardly mattered in this instance but by now she was unstoppable. I asked her, not without mischief, if she had any customers from among the refugee community.

I kept wondering how different her approach might be if she had recognised me as a priest and I toyed with the idea of identifying myself or offering her a paternal and parting blessing, just the see her reaction. I figured that if I wasn't identifiable as a priest by my demeanour and attitudes and needed a uniform to proclaim my priestly nature, then I would simply have to keep up the attitude-adjusting routine. I could have countered her attitudes and judgements and even tried a bit of evangelism but all I wanted was a quick haircut and an even quicker exit. Having a cut-throat razor skimmed over your neck and upper cheeks does not encourage dissent so I carried on complying.

The end was nigh. She lifted up the mirror and showed me my shaven neckline, keeping the mirror diplomatically low so as not to highlight my barren crown. Having murmured approval she proceeded to apply a gel called 'Dak' to my remaining crop. My mind instantly returned to greasy Brylcreemed Sunday mornings when I was a child and I shuddered inwardly in distaste. She assured me that this hair product was nothing like

Brylcreem and as my hair tended to be dry, it was the perfect hair-recipe for me and a little dab of it would do no harm, recovered memories or not.

For the first time in years I went off without telling the barber not to use hairspray or apply anything of this kind to my hair. Another recovered memory reminded me that 'Dak' was a sticky black substance used for catching wild birds. How words and products change, whatever about the end purpose. I parted with my fiver, decided against a tip, (we had covered that topic too) and walked off feeling my cranial stubble and glancing surreptitiously in shop windows. I decided it was the shortest and best haircut I had had in a very long time.

Getting a life

Difference fascinates people. We seek out the different to stimulate us, to challenge our received ideas and to disturb our routine, even if we return with relief to the cycle and the tedium of everyday life. The life of a priest is different to that of most others, so regularly, when I find myself in conversation with others, at a dinner function for example, I find myself questioned about one or other aspect of the life of a priest.

Most of us live lives of routine and regularity, so drama and difference fascinates. People express their fear of and wonder at the perceived drama in life and in priesthood, as when attending a road accident, or breaking news of a death for example. They say, 'I wouldn't like to have your job, father'. Like so many people who work in public services, the truth is that you simply get used to it, or to most of it. Like any professional, you can't invest emotionally in most situations or you would soon suffer from emotional overload and perhaps crash into burnout. There are always some situations which penetrate the professional cordon you set up and incidents involving children can crack even the most hardened professional shell.

There is a difference in priesthood in that your contact with victims and families of victims may last longer than that of the emergency services, and you may be asked in the context of ritual or otherwise, to make sense of what has happened. The reality of a busy priest's life usually precludes any dwelling on these things for a long time though, as the demands of life and work take over. The sorrow of a funeral is replaced in the mind of the priest, if not in that of the family, by the excitement of a couple preparing their marriage, or the joy of a family in baptising their child. The emotional roller-coaster continues, replacing one emotionally highly charged situation with another. The skill of a priest is to manage successfully the emotional situations he finds himself involved in, and to integrate each new experience successfully, learning all the time. To do this, a good priest needs to be emotionally well balanced with an integrated personality and to be capable of constant change.

Situations are rarely as dramatic as they seem to an outside observer. People create drama to escape from the predictability of life and to give rein to their imaginative powers. The drama of one person's life may be the daily bread of another. It is not for lack of care that a professional may not invest too much emotionally, but for reasons of sanity and well-being. No one can live a life of high emotional intensity for too long without suffering the consequences.

Weddings, funerals, christenings, sick calls, separations, celebrations and life problems of all kinds form part of the workload of a working priest. These and other situations are the intense times when people are likely to encounter a priest at work. There are however, as for everyone else, the daily chores which seem to have no end, the routine which dulls the mind and numbs the senses, and the imaginative escapes to places and situation where people are nicer and life is more exciting. There is always 'the something' which is worrying and harassing the quietened mind, and the list of things still to be done, 'when you get time'.

There is probably no other calling which gives the same variety in work situations, which is so unpredictable in terms of career, and which allows such privileged access to people at the most vulnerable and at the happiest times of their lives. There may be no other calling with the same potential for varied insight into human nature, or with the same access to the darkness and shadows of daily human existence. There is also, despite public perception, great individual freedom and, for most, the reward of people's trust and affection. If you must, 'get a life', it is at least as rewarding as most others, and as ordinary and extraordinary as human nature.

From the outside in

One of the things that constantly amaze me is the persistent misconceptions that people have regarding the life of a priest. Perhaps I once shared these idealized images myself for it is such images that used to attract people to the priesthood in large numbers. One of the first questions an enquirer will ask is, 'How many children are in your family?' When I respond that we are five boys and no girls, I am usually asked if any more of the family are priests. The answer is no. It seems that many people expect vocations to run in the family, 'like the wooden leg' as used to be said.

It is true that there were dynasties of priests from certain families in the past. These families were commonly known as 'Levitical' families. This was a reference to the tradition of service in the Old Testament priesthood and in the Temple that was the privilege and inheritance of the biblical tribe of Levi. There were priest-uncles who educated and trained their Irish nephews into priesthood because the cost of long-term education at the time was prohibitive for most parents. Cousins and siblings from some families all entered priesthood or religious life. A glance at the Diocesan Directory today shows that the days of such patterns of inherited priesthood are all but over. Few priests under the age of fifty have immediate relatives who have also followed vocations in the diocese or elsewhere. The truth of my own story is that I have no immediate family in religious life nor have I had priest-ancestors for many generations, if ever.

Another misconception is that the priest was inevitably raised in a middle-class or professional family or came from a 'strong farmer' background. It used to be said that the defining characteristics of the strong farmer were to have; a priest in the parish, a pump in the yard, a piano in the parlour, and bulled his own cows'. This idea may stem from the days when only such families could afford to train as priests. In far-off days this training often finished in a seminary on the continent, in one of the many 'Irish' Colleges or seminaries founded all over Europe in the late sixteenth and early seventeenth centuries. Between 1578 and 1680 almost thirty colleges were founded across Europe to train Irish priests for the 'home mission' in Ireland. Each student had to give a written undertaking that he would return to the difficult, harsh and often dangerous conditions of post-Reformation Ireland.

I was reminded of this recently when I saw the large medieval house that was the Irish College in Santiago in North West Spain and when I visited the site of another Irish College in Lisbon, Portugal. The official title of these institutions generally described them as colleges for the 'noble' Irish. In those days of strict social hierarchy and fixed positions in societies, the nobility or otherwise of a family was important. In our days of social mobility and equality of opportunity, such considerations seem quaint or unjust. As a priest-inheritor of the tradition of noble clergy I can only claim to have been reared simply on a smallholding of twenty acres by decent parents who had no claims or pretensions to noble blood.

Whatever about nobility of background or hereditary priestliness, one of the attributes that the priest is expected to have is a lack of worldliness; a certain innocence of the ways of the wicked world. He is expected to be easily impressed by feigned piety ('God bless you Father, you're a grand man') and to be easily persuaded by the sob-stories and lies of con-artists. It is true that many priests in the recent past came through a very sheltered upbringing and training and were undoubtedly socially naïve, at least at the outset of their ministry. It is invariably assumed that the priest, whatever his background, was always a priest and has no knowledge of what really goes on in the adult world. There is a misconception that the priest is not really of this world, that he is easily shocked and that he is not fully aware of the deviousness that can be at the heart of human dealings and behaviour.

When confronted with the priest's refusal to be manipulated by the devious, there generally follows accusations of lack of compassion and unfavourable comparisons with predecessors. There is nothing Christian, however, in allowing oneself to be conned or misled and consequently demeaned. Real compassion means much more than the occasional hand-out at the presbytery door. The perception of social innocence and lack of 'savvy' on the part of the priest also leads to the easy dismissal of anything serious that he tries to say on the grounds that he does not really understand 'real life'. 'Sure what would he know and him a priest'.

I remember being asked as a young priest, 'What time do you have to be in at?' The question betrayed an assumption that the priest lives under constant authority and supervision. 'Do you have to say Mass every day? Can a priest drink or smoke?' These questions highlight the underlying assumption that the life of a priest is very structured and is hedged around by rules and regulations, most of which are negative and about things you cannot do. The reality for priests can be very different in various workplaces but the general situation for those who work in parishes is that the average work-day is fluid and unstructured. There may be regular chores and appointments and there are certainly unexpected demands but there is also the freedom to organize most of the working day according to your own schedule. There is a certain freedom in being your own boss in the daily business of life but there is also the drawback of having no definite hours and of trying to be generally available to those in your pastoral care. Like the proverbial housewife the work of a priest is 'never done'. There is also the not inconsiderable freedom of the celibate, priest or otherwise, who does not have to negotiate the details of his or her daily life with another. Freedom is not something you might immediately associate with the life of a priest but perceptions can often be misperceptions when the view is from the outside in.

ISBN 1-41204076-0

9 781412 040761